Smart Start Read & Write

This book belongs to

Name

Writing: Barbara Allman
Content Editing: Lisa Vitarisi Mathews
Joy Evans
Copy Editing: Laurie Westrich
Art Direction: Yuki Meyer
Cover Design: Yuki Meyer
Cover Illustration: Chris Lensch
Illustration: Shirley Beckes
Design/Production: Jessica Onken

EMC 2427

Visit *teaching-standards.com* to view a correlation of this book. This is a free service.

Correlated to Current Standards

Congratulations on your purchase of some of the finest teaching materials in the world.

EVAN-MOOR CORP.
phone 1-800-777-4362, fax 1-800-777-4332.

18 Lower Ragsdale Drive, Monterey, CA 93940-5746. Printed in China.

004

CPSIA: Asia Pacific Offset Ltd, Kowloon, Hong Kong [5/2020]

Contents

How to Use This Book

Helping Your Child Become a Reader and a Writer

Children see letters and words at home, in their community, and at school. They are naturally curious about how to read and write. Many children begin by learning the alphabet and then progress to learning letter sounds. The activities in this book will help your child practice naming and writing uppercase and lowercase letters and connecting those letters to the sounds they stand for. In addition, a variety of readiness activities promote print awareness, visual discrimination, following directions, and fine motor skills.

Alphabet Stories

Each alphabet story focuses on one or more alphabet characters. You may wish to listen to the audio story with your child or read the story aloud to your child. Have your child listen for words that begin with the focus sound and look at the picture. After you finish the story, have your child retell you the story as he or she points to things in the picture that begin with the focus sound.

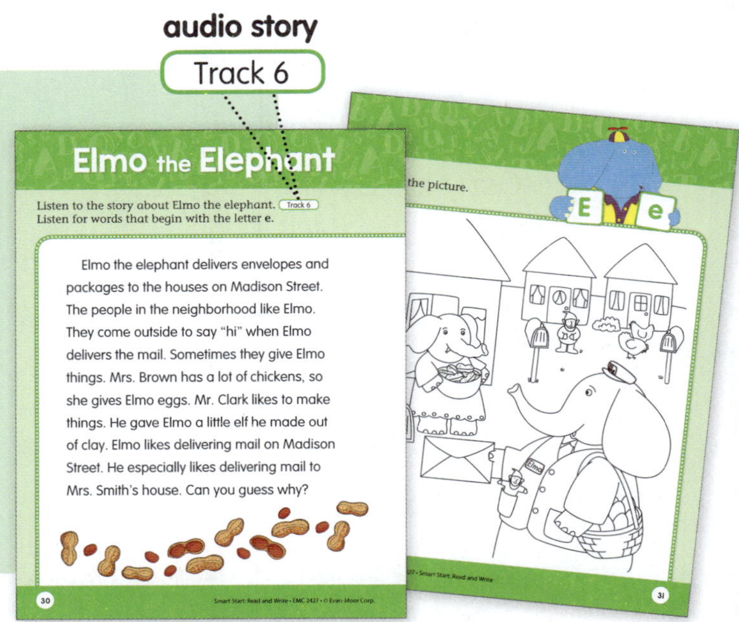

Listen for It! Activities

These activities focus on beginning letter sounds. Read aloud the directions to your child and help him or her name the pictures. If your child needs additional support as he or she completes the activity, read aloud the focus word and then name a picture as you point to it. Say, *Do these words have the same beginning sound?*

Write It! Activities

These activities focus on writing and identifying uppercase and lowercase letters. Provide your child with support and encouragement as he or she traces the letters. Point out how to use the numbers and arrows as a guide. Explain that it takes a lot of practice to learn to print, so it's okay if the letters he or she writes look different from the letters on the page.

Find It! Activities

These activities focus on identifying uppercase and lowercase letters that match and drawing a picture of something that begins with the focus sound. Provide your child with support as he or she completes the activity. Help your child think of things in his or her environment that begin with the focus sound. Provide encouragement as your child draws the picture.

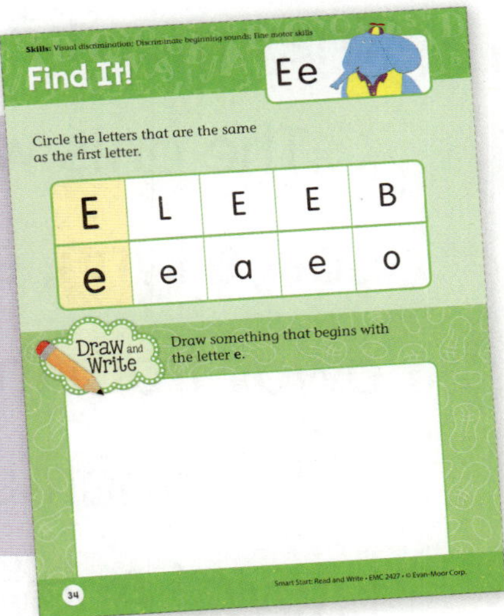

Let's Review! Activities

These activities provide an informal assessment of your child's understanding of each alphabet letter and the beginning sound it stands for, as well as his or her ability to print the upper- and lowercase letters. If your child needs additional practice, you may wish to review the pages together again, having him or her do the activities orally and using his or her finger to trace each letter.

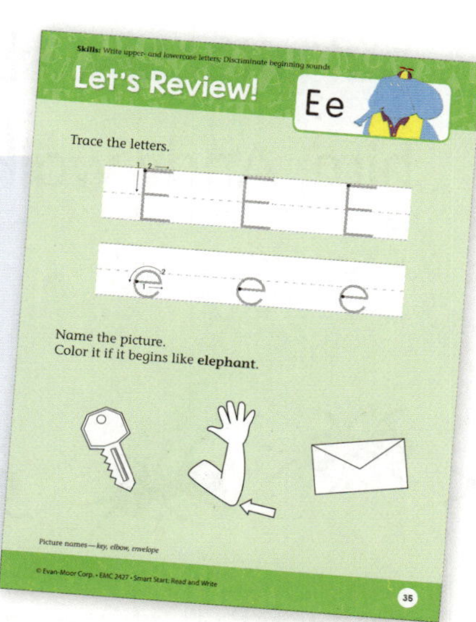

Andy the Ant

Listen to the story about Andy the ant. Track 2
Listen for words that begin with the letter **a**.

One afternoon, Lynn sat under an apple tree and ate a crunchy red apple. She watched the busy ants on the anthill right beside her. They marched up the hill in a little black line.

The ants were so busy that they didn't even notice Lynn, except for one ant that wandered away from the hill and crawled up her arm.

Lynn named the ant "Andy." She didn't know if Andy was lost or just looking for food, but after she shared some of her apple with him, Andy walked back home.

Skills: Write upper- and lowercase letters; Discriminate beginning sounds

Let's Review!

Trace the letters.

Name the picture.
Color it if it begins like **bear**.

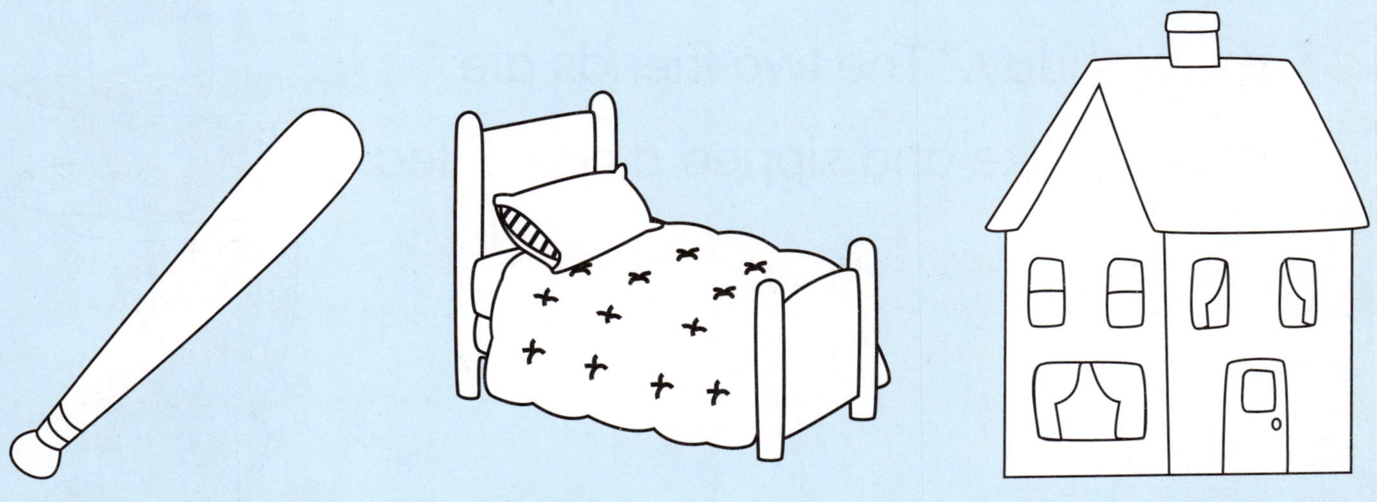

Picture names—*bat, bed, house*

Callie the Cat

Listen to the story about Callie the cat. Track 4
Listen for words that begin with the letter **c**.

Callie the cat heard the clock strike four o'clock. It was time for a cup of tea. She closed her book and picked up her cane. On her way to the kitchen, she met Miss Mouse. Her little friend was carrying a cupcake with a candle in it. "Happy birthday!" said Miss Mouse.

Callie cried out, "What a nice surprise! Thank you for remembering my birthday." The two friends ate the cupcake and sipped a cup of tea.

Color the picture.

Skills: Discriminate beginning sounds; Fine motor skills

Listen for It!

Name the picture.
Circle it if it begins with the same sound as **cat**.

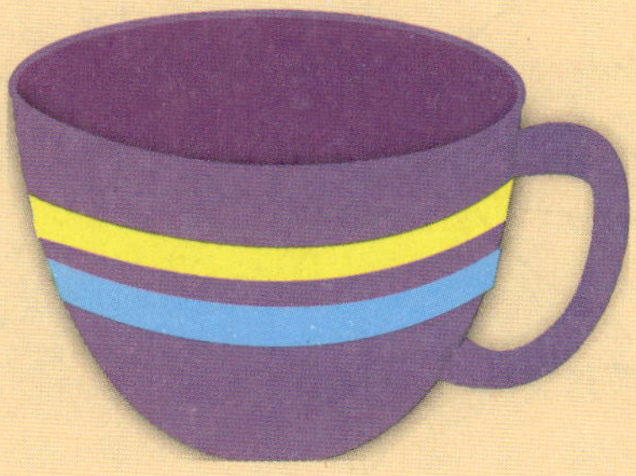

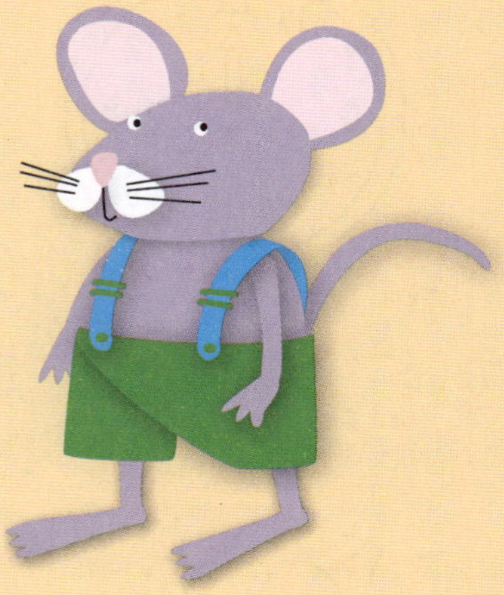

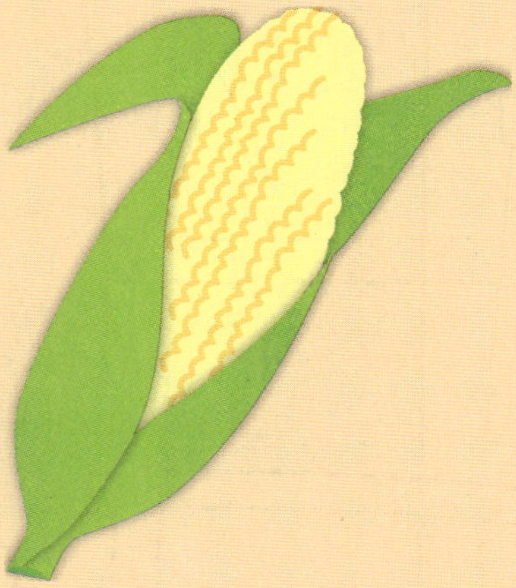

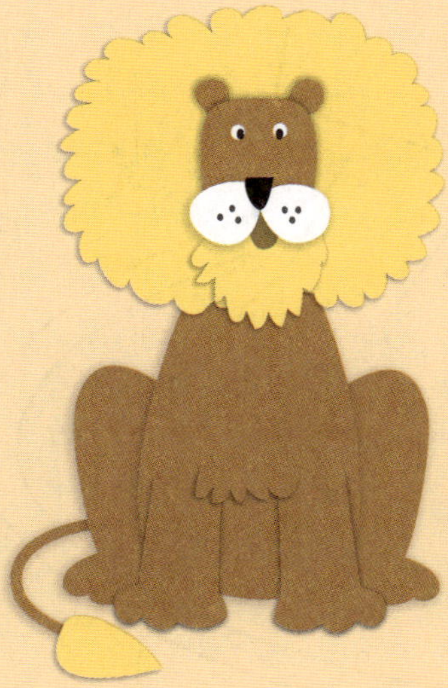

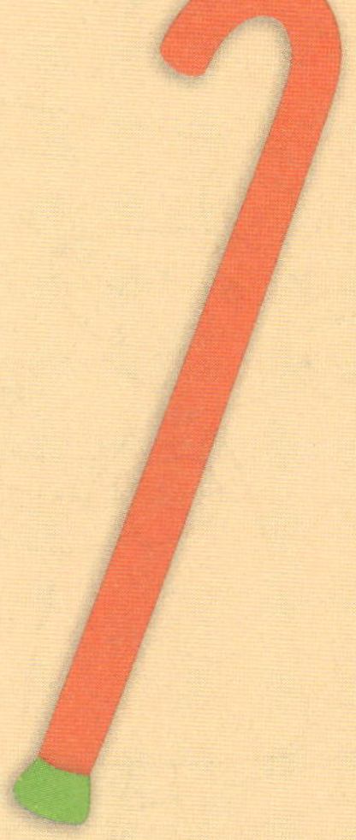

Picture names—*cup, mouse, corn, lion, cane*

Skills: Write upper- and lowercase letters; Fine motor skills; Visual discrimination

Write It!

Trace the letters.

Find the big **C** and the little **c**.
Circle them.

Skills: Visual discrimination; Discriminate beginning sounds; Fine motor skills

Find It!

Circle the letters that are the same as the first letter.

C	D	C	P	C
c	p	c	c	d

Draw something that begins with the letter **c**.

Let's Review!

Trace the letters.

Name the picture.
Color it if it begins like **cat**.

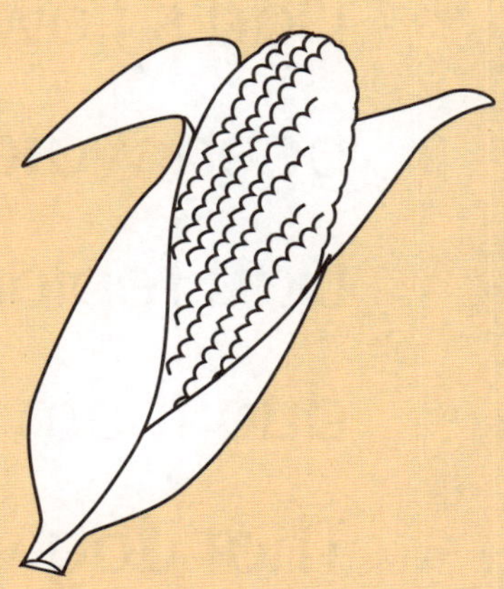

Picture names—*cup, mouse, corn*

Digger the Dog

Listen to the story about Digger the dog. Track 5
Listen for words that begin with the letter **d**.

I have a dog named "Digger." I'll tell you how he got his name. It all started in our backyard. On Saturdays, Dad digs holes to plant flowers in the garden, and I teach Digger tricks. Digger learned to roll over in one day! Dad was happy that Digger was such a fast learner until he came home from work and saw his garden. Digger had dug up all of Dad's flowers. Dad said Digger must have been watching him work in the garden. Dad replanted the flowers, but Digger dug them up again. Dad said, "Oh no! That dog won't stop digging! He's a digger!" And that's how Digger got his name.

Color the picture.

Skills: Discriminate beginning sounds; Fine motor skills

Listen for It!

Name the picture.
Circle it if it begins with the same sound as **dog**.

Picture names—*kite, door, dinosaur, duck, umbrella*

Skills: Write upper- and lowercase letters; Fine motor skills; Visual discrimination

Write It!

Trace the letters.

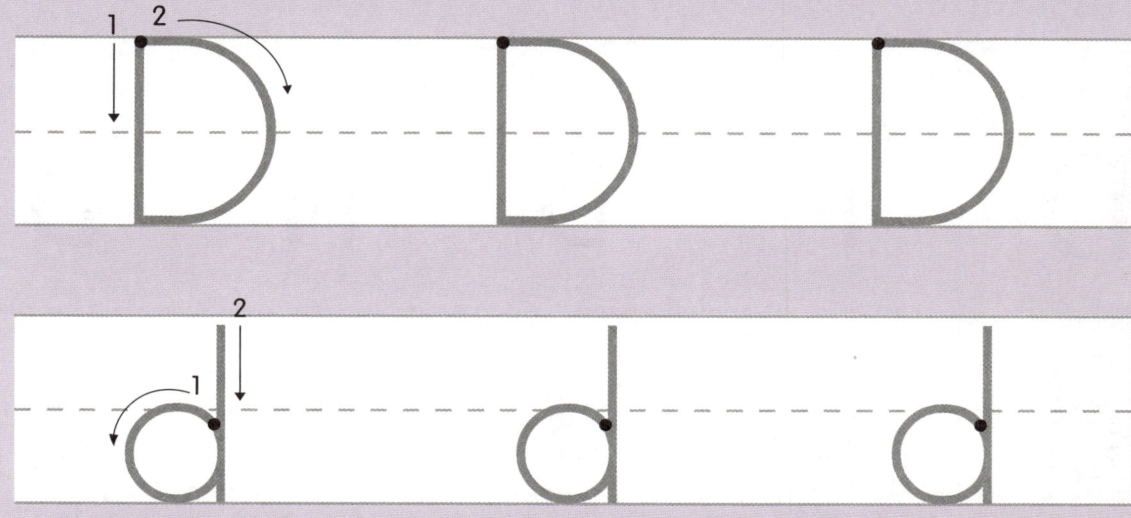

Find the big **D** and the little **d**.
Circle them.

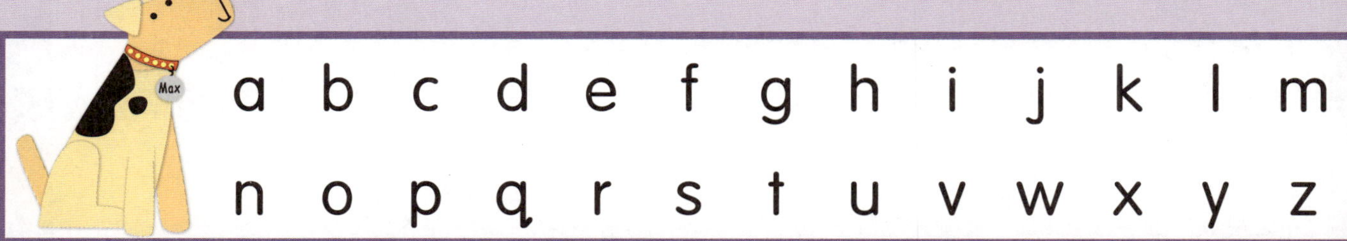

Skills: Visual discrimination; Discriminate beginning sounds; Fine motor skills

Find It!

Circle the letters that are the same as the first letter.

D	P	D	N	D
d	d	a	l	d

Draw something that begins with the letter **d**.

Skills: Write upper- and lowercase letters; Discriminate beginning sounds

Let's Review!

Trace the letters.

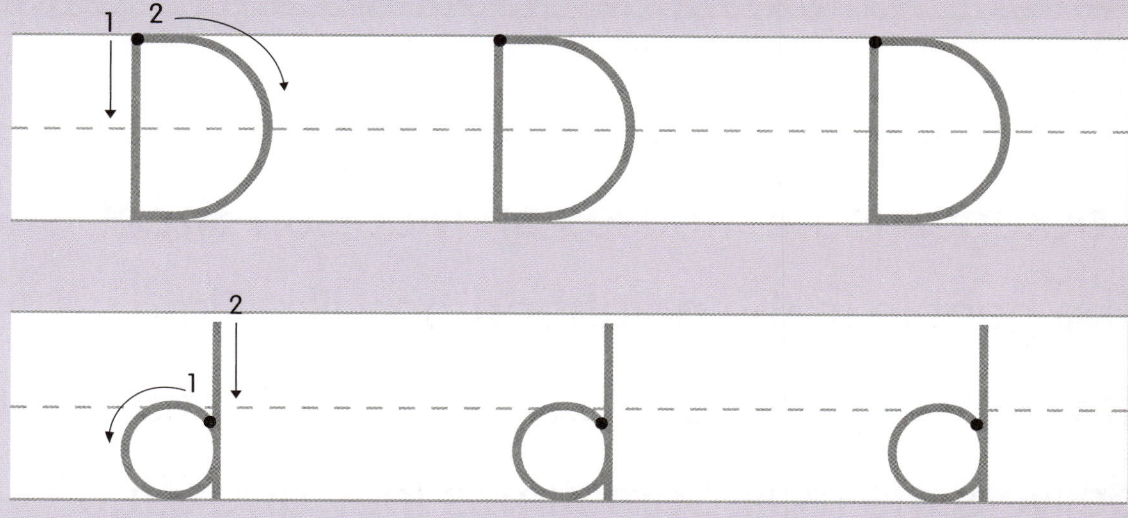

Name the picture.
Color it if it begins like **dog**.

Picture names—*umbrella, duck, door*

Elmo the Elephant

Listen to the story about Elmo the elephant. Track 6
Listen for words that begin with the letter **e**.

Elmo the elephant delivers envelopes and packages to the houses on Madison Street. The people in the neighborhood like Elmo. They come outside to say "hi" when Elmo delivers the mail. Sometimes they give Elmo things. Mrs. Brown has a lot of chickens, so she gives Elmo eggs. Mr. Clark likes to make things. He gave Elmo a little elf he made out of clay. Elmo likes delivering mail on Madison Street. He especially likes delivering mail to Mrs. Smith's house. Can you guess why?

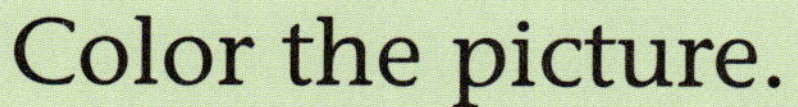

Color the picture.

Listen for It!

Name the picture.
Circle it if it begins with the same sound as **elephant**.

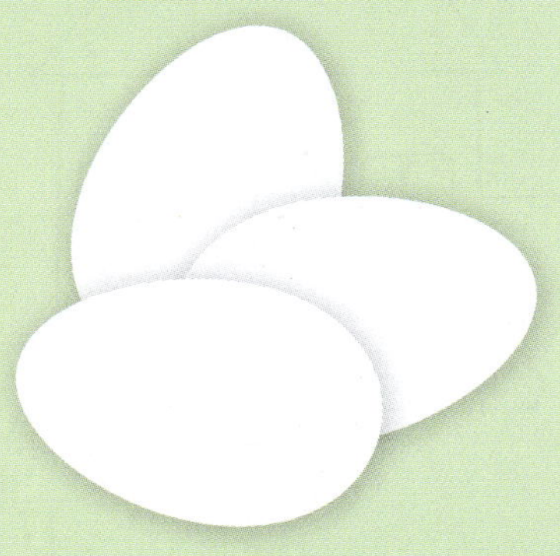

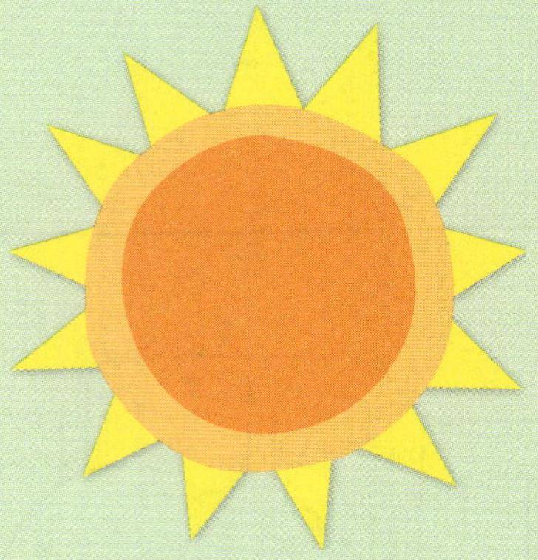

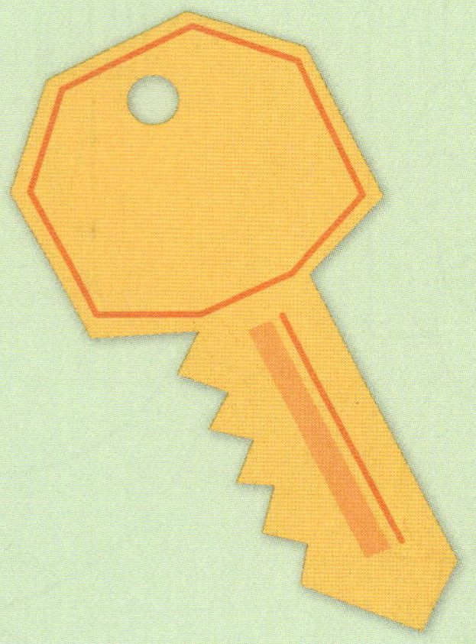

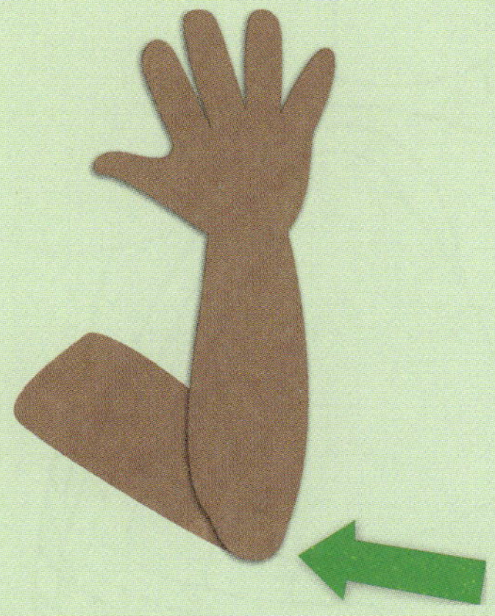

Picture names—*eggs, sun, key, elbow, envelope*

Skills: Write upper- and lowercase letters; Fine motor skills; Visual discrimination

Write It!

Trace the letters.

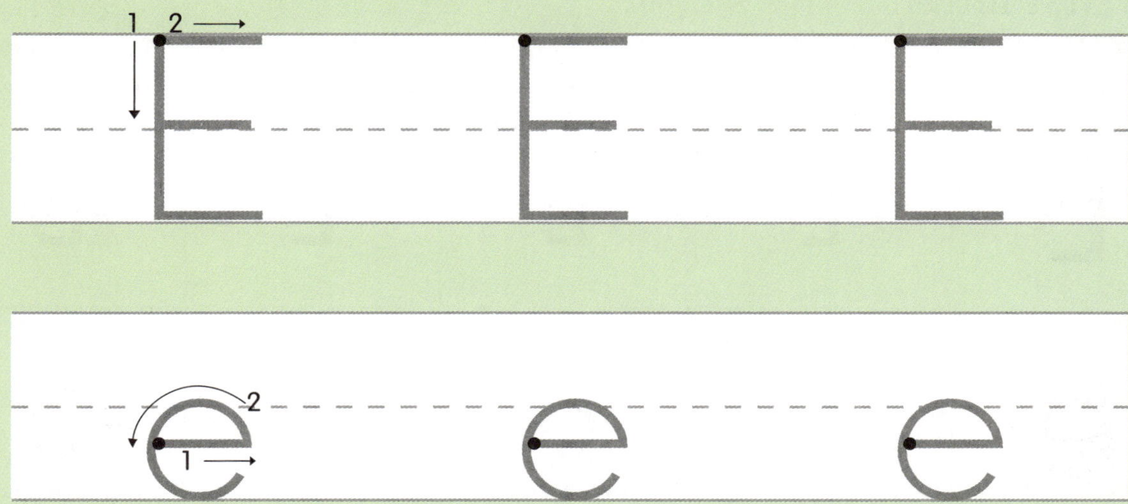

Find the big **E** and the little **e**.
Circle them.

Skills: Visual discrimination; Discriminate beginning sounds; Fine motor skills

Find It!

Circle the letters that are the same as the first letter.

E	L	E	E	B
e	e	a	e	o

Draw and Write

Draw something that begins with the letter **e**.

Skills: Write upper- and lowercase letters; Discriminate beginning sounds

Let's Review!

Trace the letters.

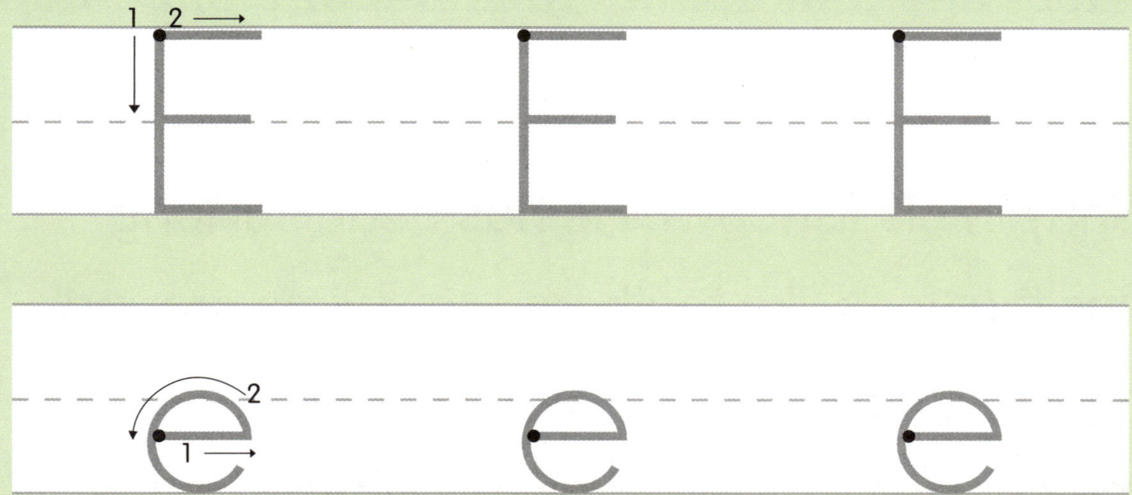

Name the picture.
Color it if it begins like **elephant**.

Picture names—*key, elbow, envelope*

Finny the Fish

Listen to the story about Finny the fish. Track 7
Listen for words that begin with the letter **f**.

Finny the fish is a fun pet. I like to watch Finny in his fishbowl. He has beautiful long fins that look like feathers. He swims around his bowl through the green seaweed and into the rock cave. Sometimes Finny hides in the cave and I can't see him. But when it's time to eat, he swims to the top of the bowl. He looks up at me and waits for his fish food sprinkles. I like taking care of Finny the fish. He is a fun pet.

Color the picture.

Skills: Discriminate beginning sounds; Fine motor skills

Listen for It!

Name the picture.
Circle it if it begins with the same sound as **fish**.

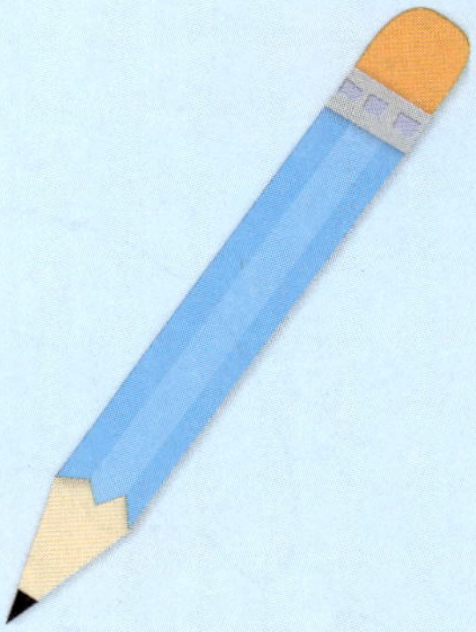

Picture names—*feather, pencil, five, duck, fox*

Skills: Write upper- and lowercase letters; Fine motor skills; Visual discrimination

Write It!

Trace the letters.

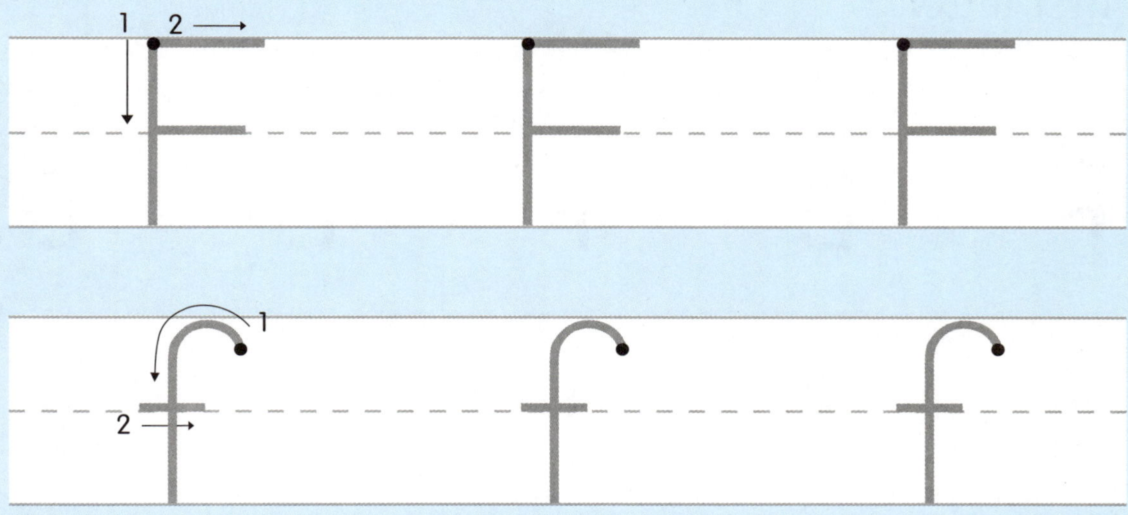

Find the big **F** and the little **f**.
Circle them.

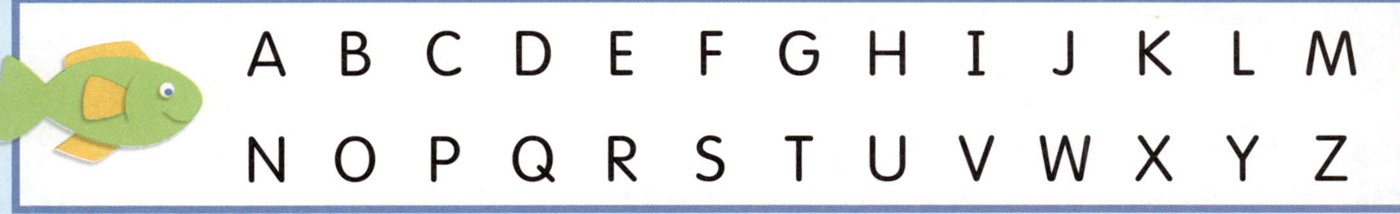

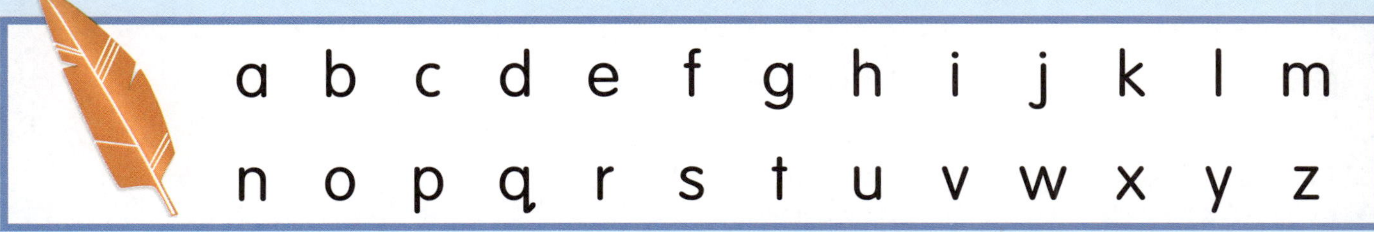

Skills: Visual discrimination; Discriminate beginning sounds; Fine motor skills

Find It!

Circle the letters that are the same as the first letter.

F	B	F	F	E
f	d	l	f	f

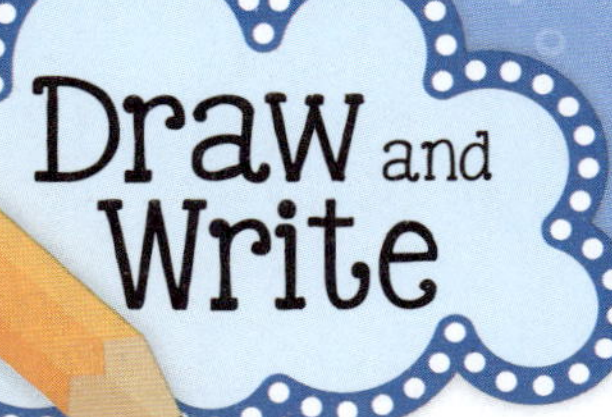

Draw something that begins with the letter **f**.

Skills: Write upper- and lowercase letters; Discriminate beginning sounds

Let's Review!

Trace the letters.

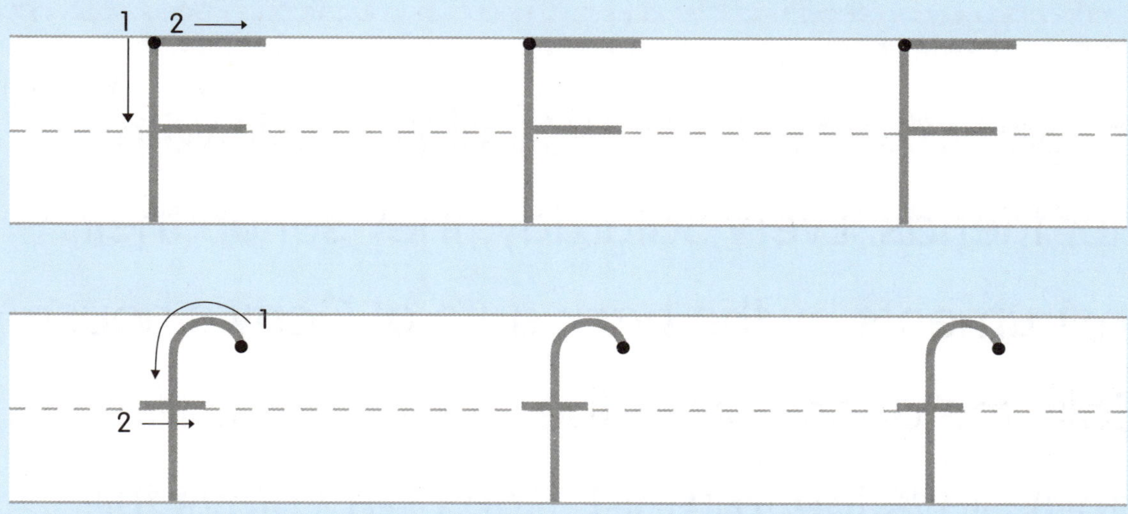

Name the picture.
Color it if it begins like **fish**.

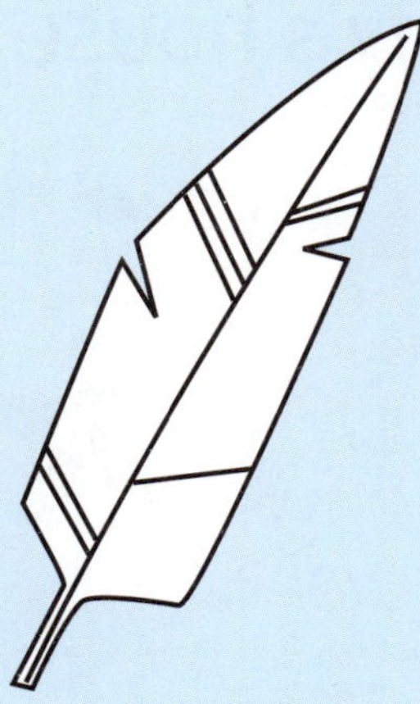

Picture names—*duck, feather, fox*

Gerty the Gorilla

Listen to the story about Gerty the gorilla. Track 8
Listen for words that begin with the letter **g**.

Gerty the gorilla likes to play music with her friends. Every Saturday, they set up their instruments by the back gate at Gerty's house. Sally the goose plays the guitar. Alfred the goat plays the trumpet, and Gerty plays the drum. Gerty's neighbors love to listen to Gerty and her friends play music. They dance and sing and say, "Go Gerty! Go Gerty!" Saturdays at Gerty's house are fun!

Color the picture.

Go Gerty!

Skills: Discriminate beginning sounds; Fine motor skills

Listen for It!

Name the picture.
Circle it if it begins with the same sound as **gorilla**.

Picture names—*gate, guitar, bed, goat, nine*

Skills: Write upper- and lowercase letters; Fine motor skills; Visual discrimination

Write It!

Trace the letters.

Find the big **G** and the little **g**.
Circle them.

Skills: Visual discrimination; Discriminate beginning sounds; Fine motor skills

Find It!

Circle the letters that are the same as the first letter.

G	G	O	D	G
g	f	g	b	g

Draw and Write

Draw something that begins with the letter **g**.

Let's Review!

Trace the letters.

Name the picture.
Color it if it begins like **gorilla**.

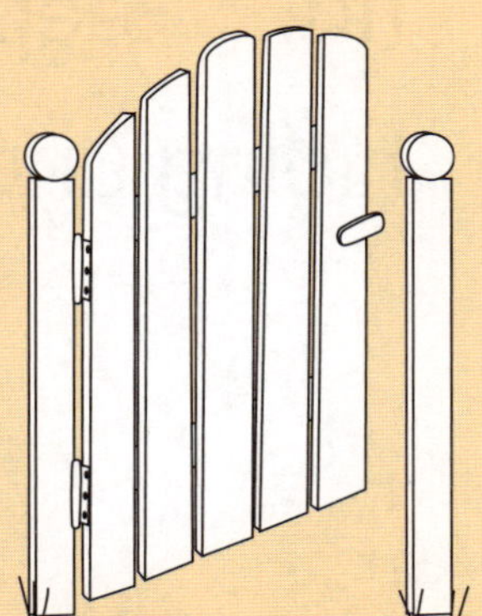

Picture names—*goat, bed, gate*

Hannah the Hen

Listen to the story about Hannah the hen. Track 9
Listen for words that begin with the letter **h**.

Hannah the hen was going to take her chicks for a walk. She counted them, "1, 2, 3, 4...where is number 5?" Hannah asked Mrs. Horse if she had seen the chick. "Neigh," said the horse. Hannah asked Mrs. Cow if she had seen the chick. "Moo!" said the cow. Hannah thought she would go out to look for her chick. So she reached for her hat. "Peep!" There was chick number 5, hiding under Hannah's hat!

Color the picture.

Skills: Discriminate beginning sounds; Fine motor skills

Listen for It!

Name the picture.
Circle it if it begins with the same sound as **hen**.

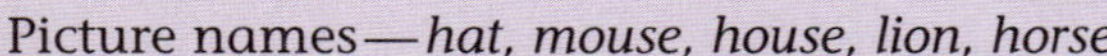

Picture names—*hat, mouse, house, lion, horse*

Skills: Write upper- and lowercase letters; Fine motor skills; Visual discrimination

Write It!

Trace the letters.

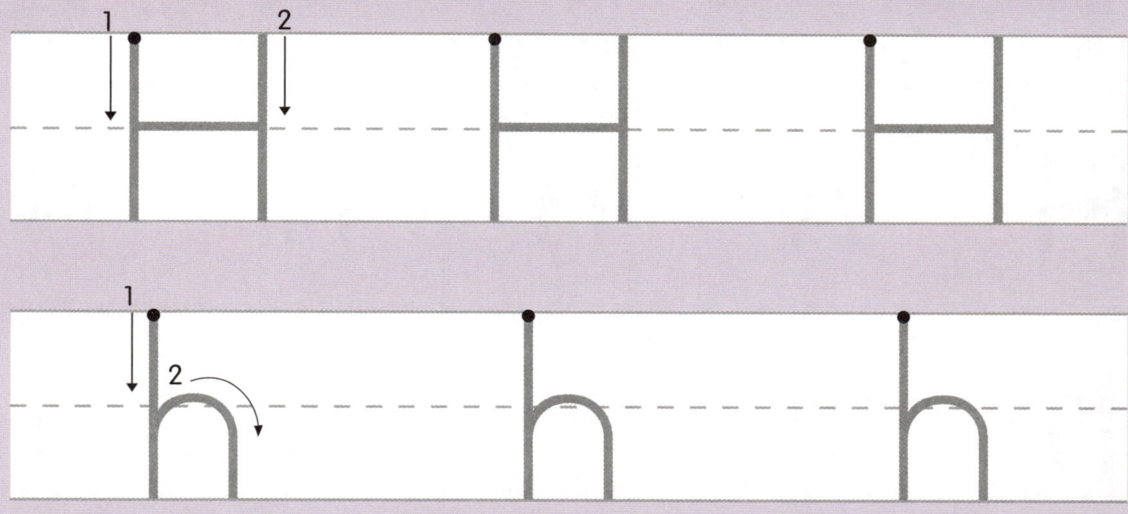

Find the big **H** and the little **h**.
Circle them.

Skills: Visual discrimination; Discriminate beginning sounds; Fine motor skills

Find It!

Circle the letters that are the same as the first letter.

H	A	H	H	N
h	b	h	n	h

Draw something that begins with the letter **h**.

Skills: Write upper- and lowercase letters; Discriminate beginning sounds

Let's Review!

Trace the letters.

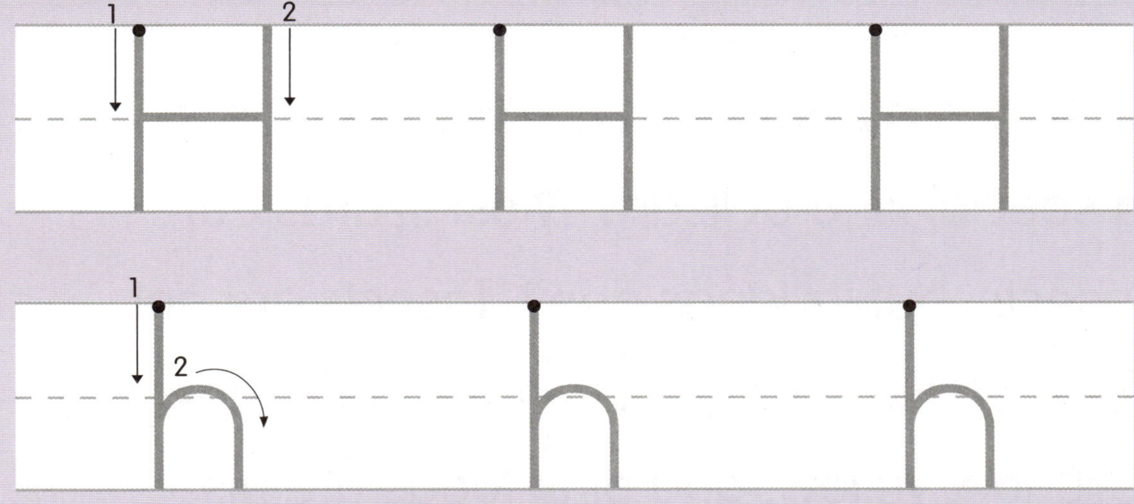

Name the picture.
Color it if it begins like **hen**.

Picture names—*hat, house, mouse*

Izzy the Iguana

Listen to the story about Izzy the iguana. Track 10
Listen for words that begin with the letter **i**.

Izzy is a baby iguana. An iguana is a special kind of lizard. Most lizards eat insects, but iguanas don't. Insects are not for Izzy! He eats flowers, fruits, and leaves. Orange, yellow, and pink foods are his favorites. Iguanas grow slowly, but Izzy is getting bigger inch by inch. His scaly tail is getting longer, and his pointy scales are growing taller. When Izzy is two years old, he will be a full-grown iguana.

Color the picture.

Skills: Discriminate beginning sounds; Fine motor skills

Listen for It!

Name the picture.
Circle it if it begins with the same sound as **iguana**.

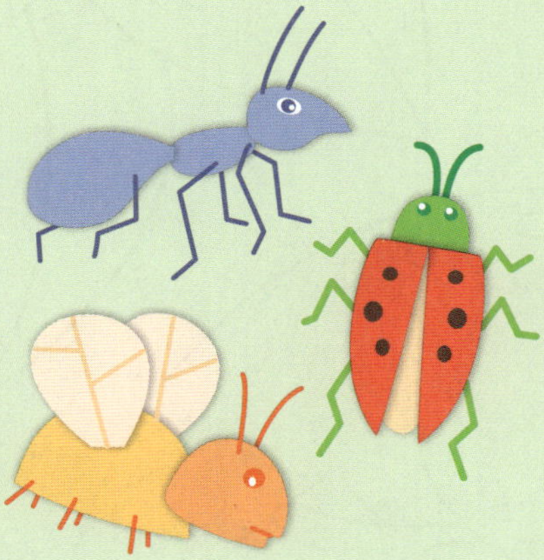

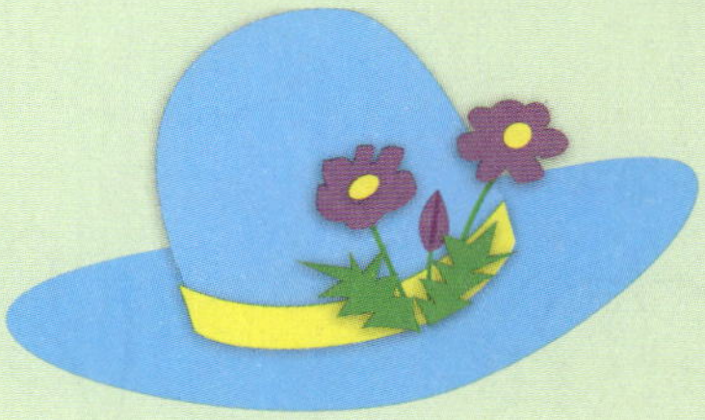

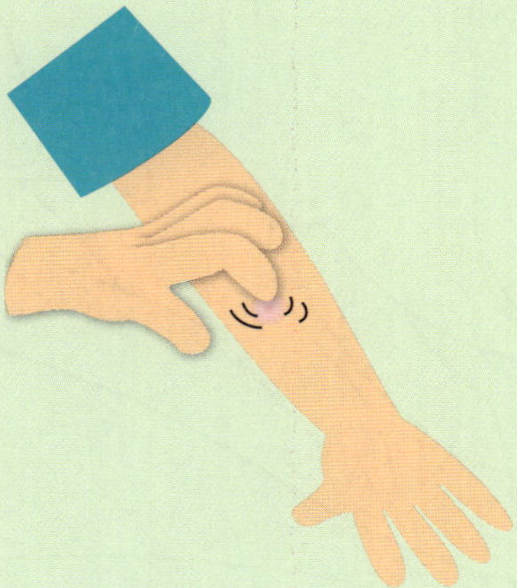

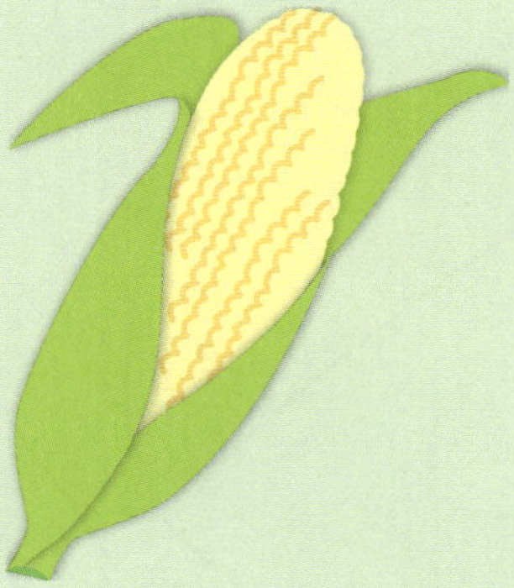

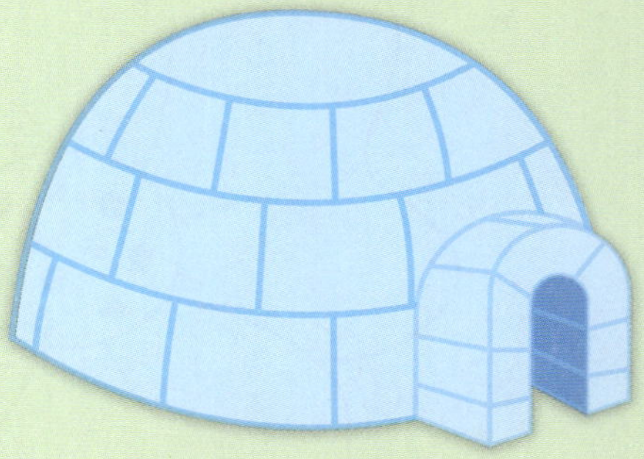

Picture names—*insects, hat, itch, corn, igloo*

Skills: Write upper- and lowercase letters; Fine motor skills; Visual discrimination

Write It!

Trace the letters.

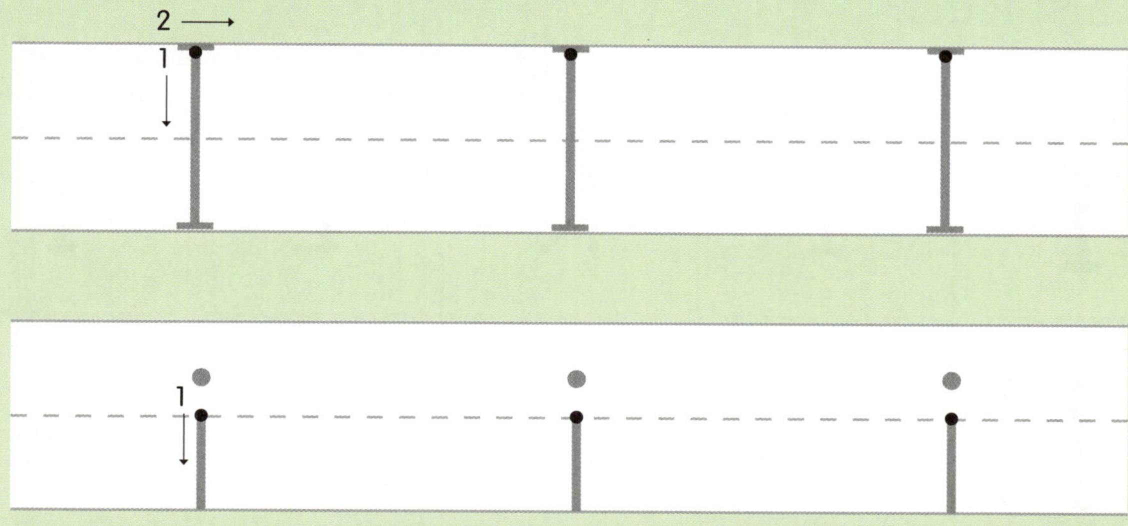

Find the big **I** and the little **i**.
Circle them.

Skills: Visual discrimination; Discriminate beginning sounds; Fine motor skills

Find It!

Circle the letters that are the same as the first letter.

I	I	K	L	I
i	b	i	i	e

Draw and Write

Draw something that begins with the letter **i**.

Skills: Write upper- and lowercase letters; Discriminate beginning sounds

Let's Review!

Trace the letters.

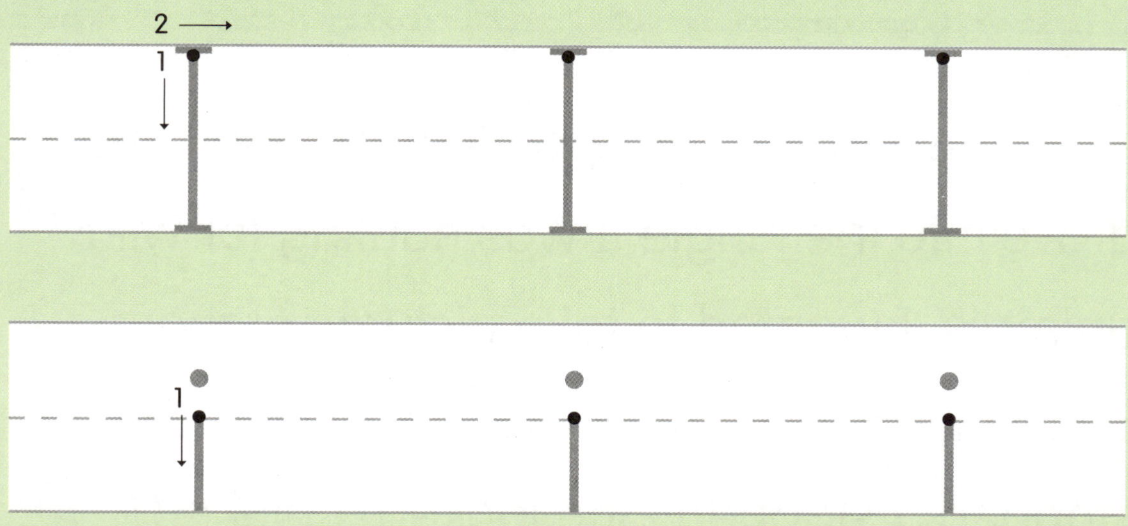

Name the picture.
Color it if it begins like **iguana**.

Picture names—*igloo, hat, insects*

Jackie the Jaguar

Listen to the story about Jackie the jaguar. Track 11
Listen for words that begin with the letter **j**.

One morning, I jumped into my jeep and drove into the jungle. I was hunting for wild animals. I wanted to take pictures of them. Suddenly, there was Jackie the jaguar. She stopped. I stopped. She looked. I looked. She growled. I screamed. She ran. I took a picture. I was surprised when I got home and found out that all I had was a picture of her tail!

Color the picture.

Skills: Discriminate beginning sounds; Fine motor skills

Listen for It!

Name the picture.
Circle it if it begins with the same sound as **jaguar**.

Picture names—*jeep, cow, jam, jet, apple*

Skills: Write upper- and lowercase letters; Fine motor skills; Visual discrimination

Write It!

Trace the letters.

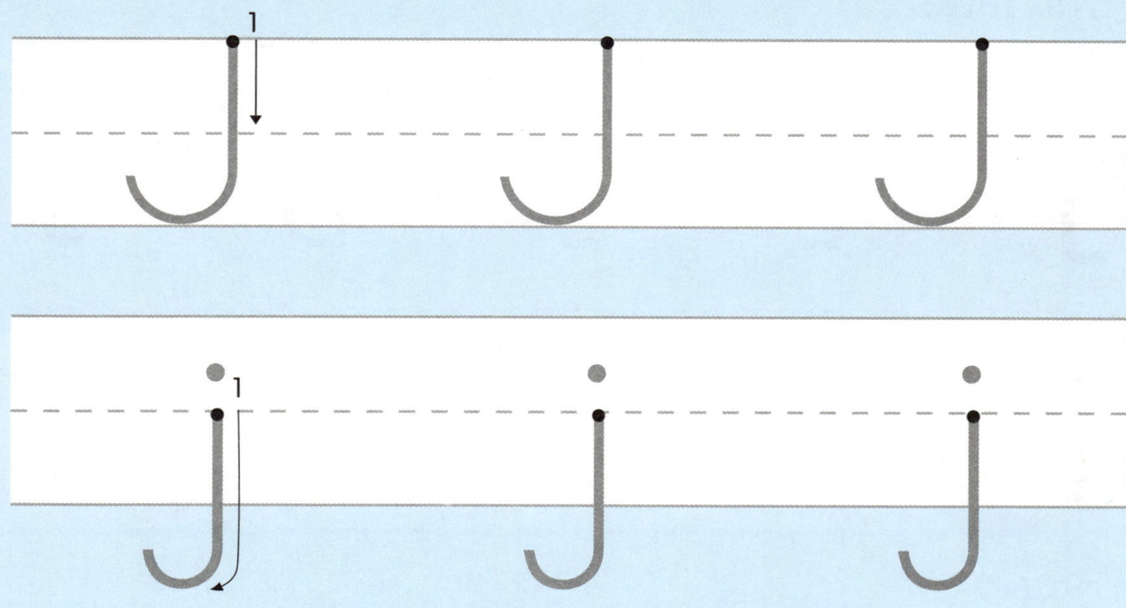

Find the big **J** and the little **j**.
Circle them.

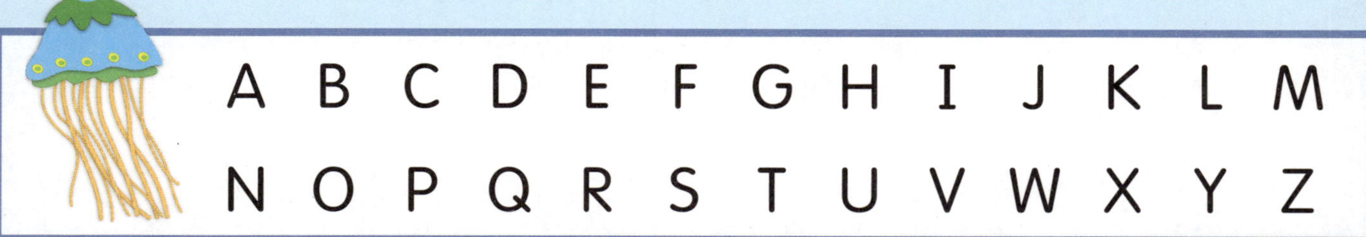

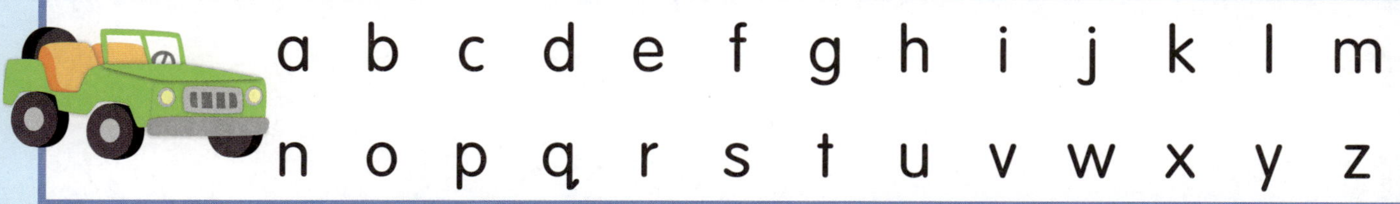

Skills: Visual discrimination; Discriminate beginning sounds; Fine motor skills

Find It!

Circle the letters that are the same as the first letter.

J	L	J	D	J
j	g	j	k	j

Draw and Write

Draw something that begins with the letter **j**.

Skills: Write upper- and lowercase letters; Discriminate beginning sounds

Let's Review!

Trace the letters.

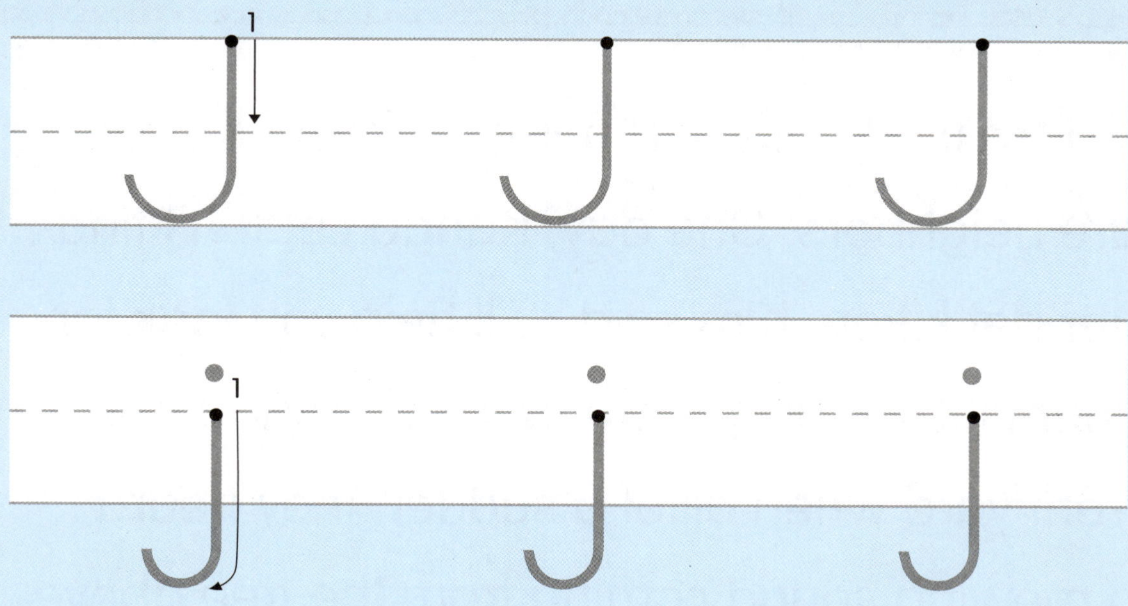

Name the picture.
Color it if it begins like **jaguar**.

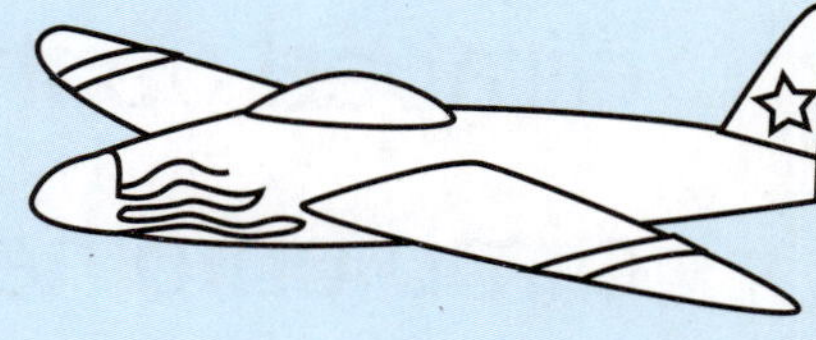

Picture names—*cow, jam, jet*

Kim the Koala

Listen to the story about Kim the koala. Track 12
Listen for words that begin with the letter **k**.

Kim the koala and her best friend Kanga are neighbors. One day, Kanga couldn't find her pet kitten. Kim said, "I'll help you look for your kitten." They were looking around the front yard when all of a sudden they heard a mewing sound coming from the tree above them. Kanga's kitten was stuck in a tree! Kanga tried to get her kitten down from the tree, but she couldn't jump high enough to reach it. Kim the koala had an idea. She climbed up the tree. Kim told the kitten to climb onto her back and hold on, like baby koalas do. Then Kim brought Kanga's kitten down from the tree.

Color the picture.

Skills: Discriminate beginning sounds; Fine motor skills

Listen for It!

Name the picture.
Circle it if it begins with the same sound as **koala**.

Picture names—*kitten, goat, five, key, king*

Skills: Write upper- and lowercase letters; Fine motor skills; Visual discrimination

Write It!

Trace the letters.

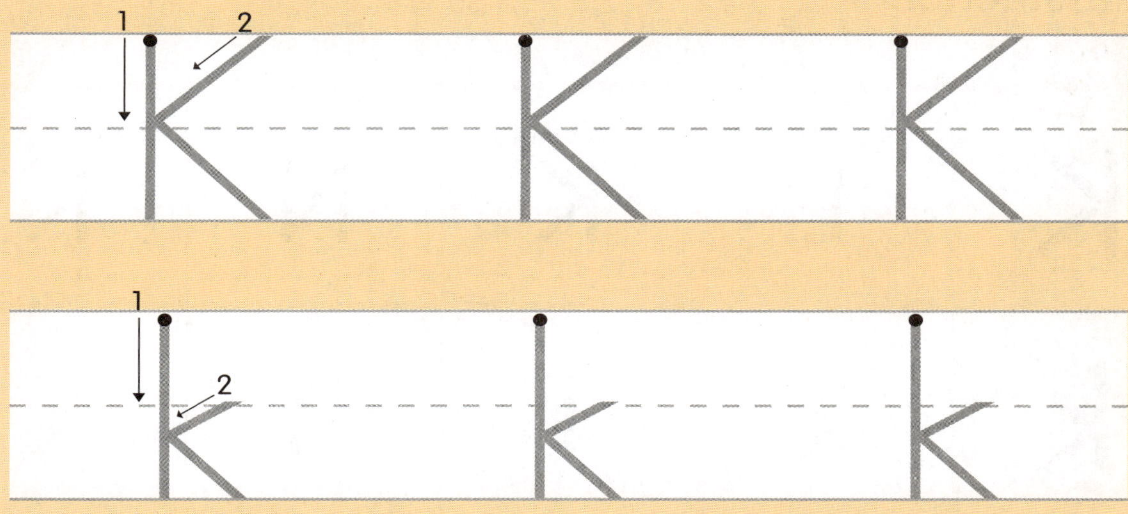

Find the big **K** and the little **k**.
Circle them.

Skills: Visual discrimination; Discriminate beginning sounds; Fine motor skills

Find It!

Circle the letters that are the same as the first letter.

K	L	K	N	K
k	k	i	h	k

Draw and Write

Draw something that begins with the letter **k**.

Skills: Write upper- and lowercase letters; Discriminate beginning sounds

Let's Review!

Trace the letters.

Name the picture.
Color it if it begins like **koala**.

Picture names—*key, goat, kite*

Lucy the Lamb

Listen to the story about Lucy the lamb. Track 13
Listen for words that begin with the letter **l**.

I have two pets. They are very different. Lucy has wool and Lisa has wings. Lucy is big and Lisa is little. Lucy has four legs and Lisa has six legs. Lucy lives outside in the barn and Lisa lives inside the house with me. There is one thing that is the same about my pets. Both of their names begin with the letter L. Can you guess which one is Lucy and which one is Lisa?

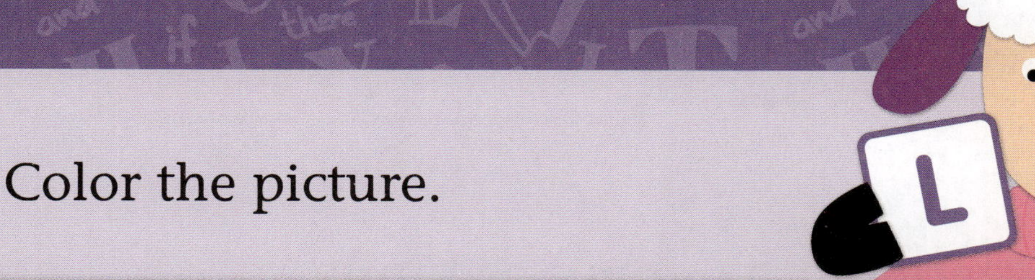

Color the picture.

Skills: Discriminate beginning sounds; Fine motor skills

Listen for It!

Name the picture.
Circle it if it begins with the same sound as **lamb**.

Picture names—*cup, ladder, bat, lion, leaf*

Skills: Write upper- and lowercase letters; Fine motor skills; Visual discrimination

Write It!

Trace the letters.

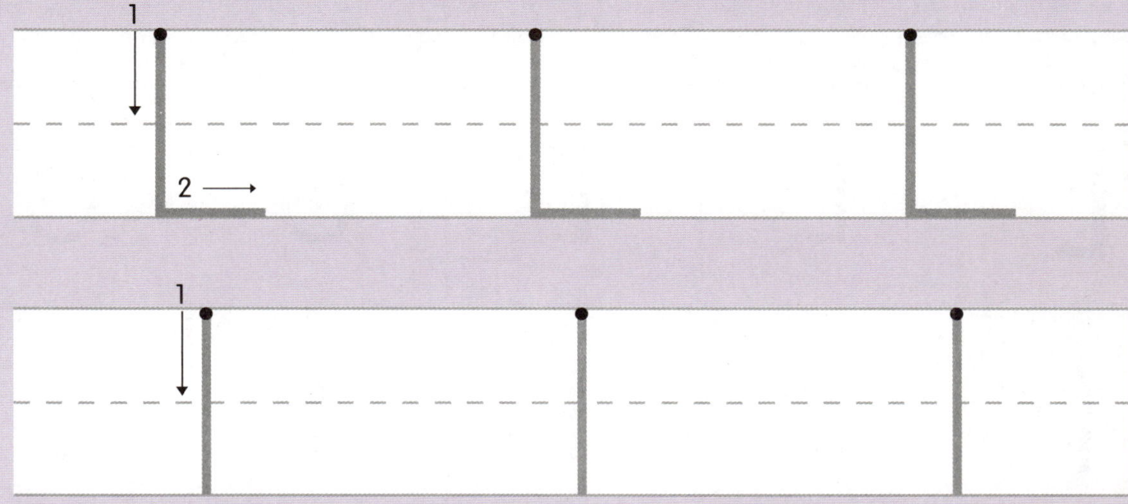

Find the big **L** and the little **l**.
Circle them.

Skills: Visual discrimination; Discriminate beginning sounds; Fine motor skills

Find It!

Circle the letters that are the same as the first letter.

L	L	L	G	G
l	d	l	l	i

Draw and Write

Draw something that begins with the letter **l**.

Skills: Write upper- and lowercase letters; Discriminate beginning sounds

Let's Review!

Trace the letters.

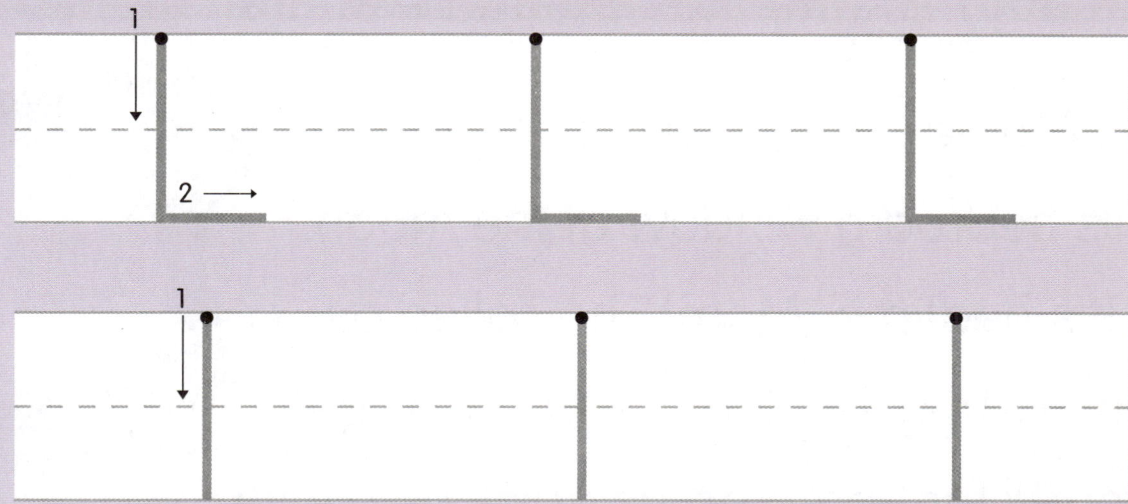

Name the picture.
Color it if it begins like **lamb**.

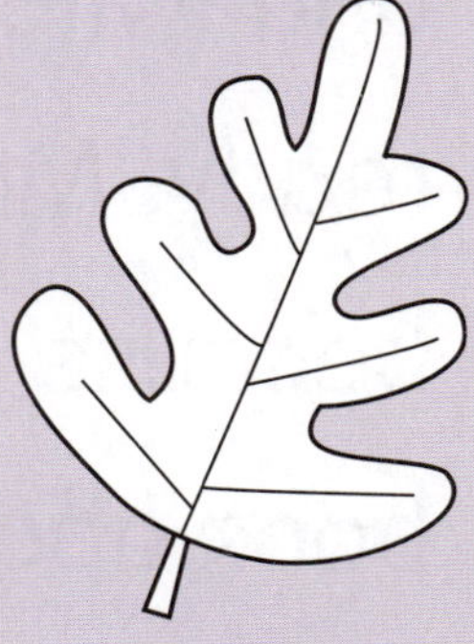

Picture names—*cup, lion, leaf*

Mortie the Mouse

Listen to the story about Mortie the mouse. Track 14
Listen for words that begin with the letter **m**.

Mortie the mouse looked out his bedroom window at the moon. "It's bedtime, Mom!" he called as he rushed into the bathroom to get ready for bed. And as quick as a wink, Mortie washed his face, brushed his teeth, combed his whiskers, and scurried back into his bedroom. Mortie looked into the mirror and twitched his nose in excitement. "I'm ready, Mom!" he called. Mortie loves bedtime because his mom always reads his favorite book about the moon. Mortie listened quietly as his mom read. "Goodnight, Moon," he said as he drifted off to sleep.

Color the picture.

Skills: Discriminate beginning sounds; Fine motor skills

Listen for It!

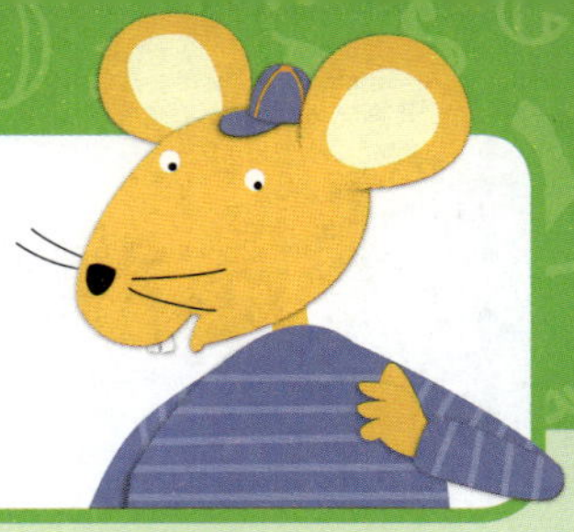

Name the picture.
Circle it if it begins with the same sound as **mouse**.

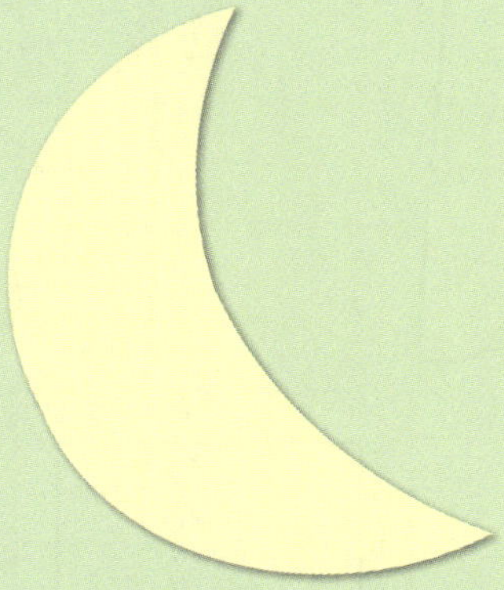

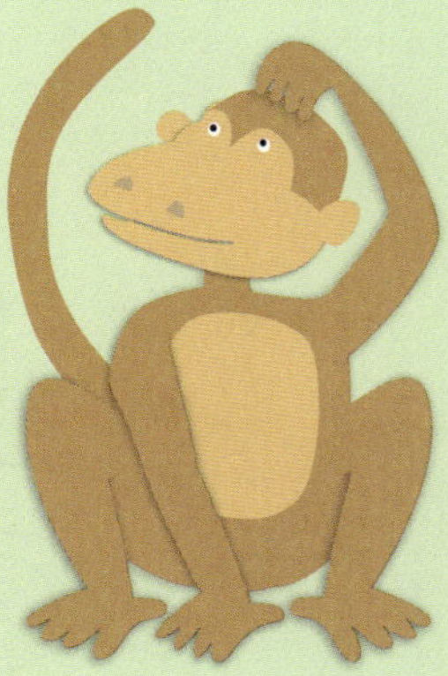

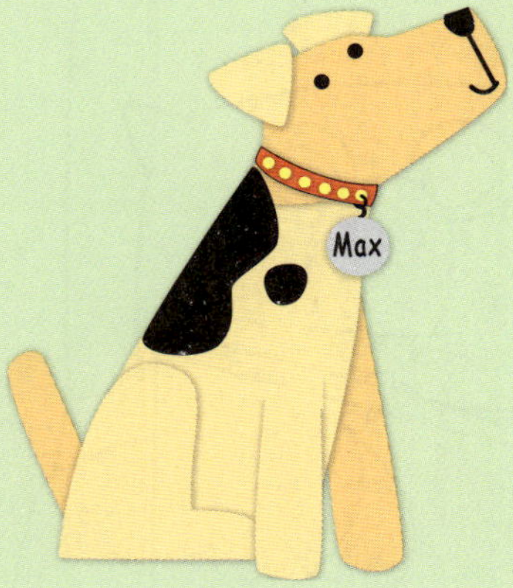

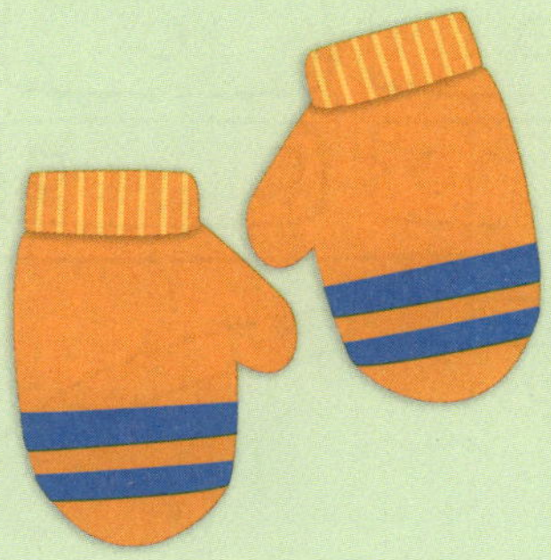

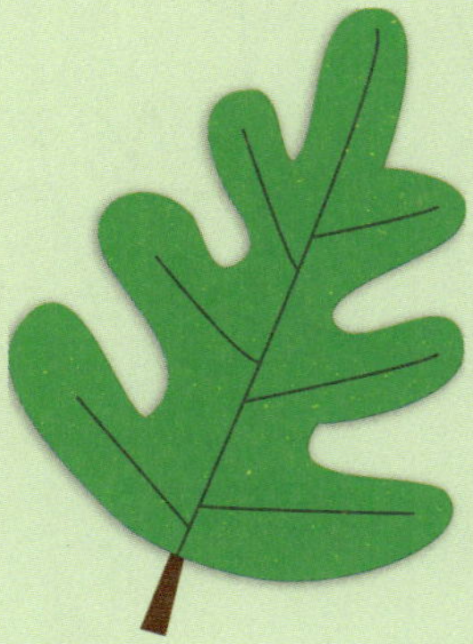

Picture names—*moon, monkey, dog, mittens, leaf*

Skills: Write upper- and lowercase letters; Fine motor skills; Visual discrimination

Write It!

Trace the letters.

Find the big **M** and the little **m**.
Circle them.

Skills: Visual discrimination; Discriminate beginning sounds; Fine motor skills

Find It!

Circle the letters that are the same as the first letter.

M	M	D	M	N
m	r	p	m	m

Draw and Write

Draw something that begins with the letter **m**.

Skills: Write upper- and lowercase letters; Discriminate beginning sounds

Let's Review!

Trace the letters.

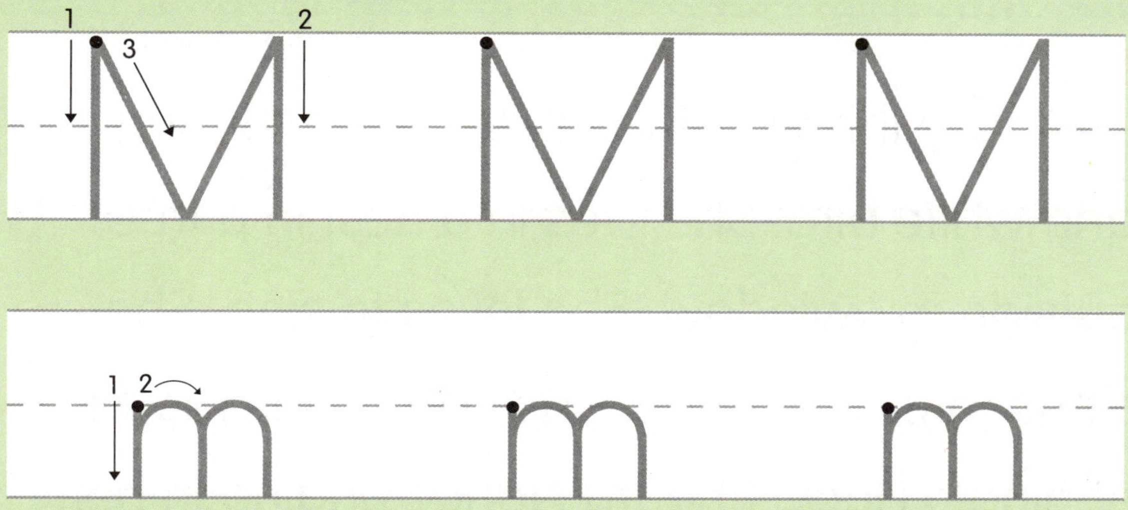

Name the picture.
Color it if it begins like **mouse**.

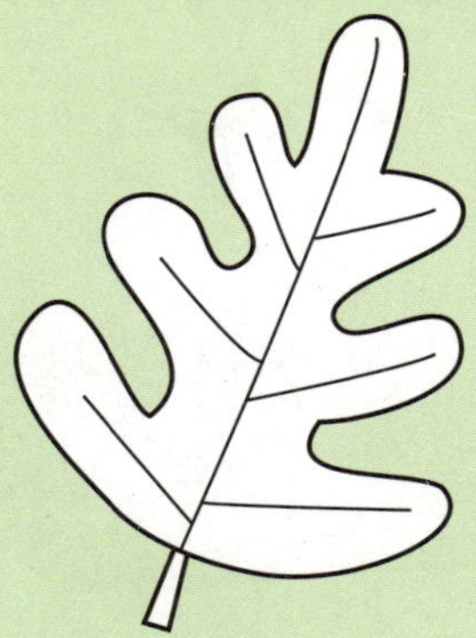

Picture names—*mittens, leaf, monkey*

Nancy the Nightingale

Listen to the story about Nancy the nightingale. Track 15
Listen for words that begin with the letter **n**.

Nancy the nightingale is a pretty brown and white bird. She lives in a nest in a tree outside my window. She loves to sing. She sings morning, noon, and night. This morning at nine o'clock, I heard Nancy singing in her nest. When she stopped, I sang a little song back to her. But before I finished singing my song, she flew away! Maybe Nancy the nightingale likes her own songs best.

Color the picture.

Listen for It!

Name the picture.
Circle it if it begins with the same sound as **nightingale**.

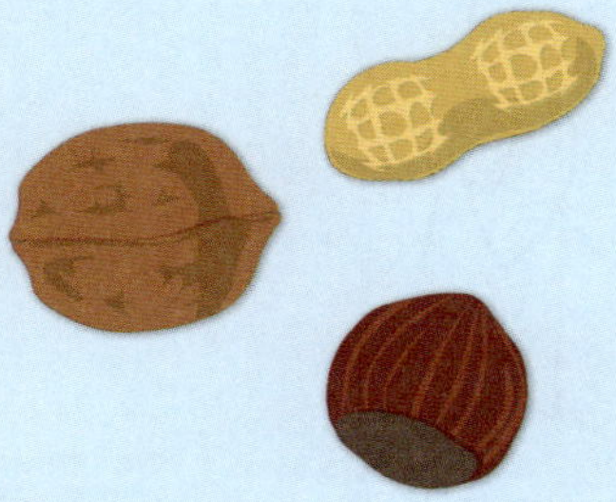

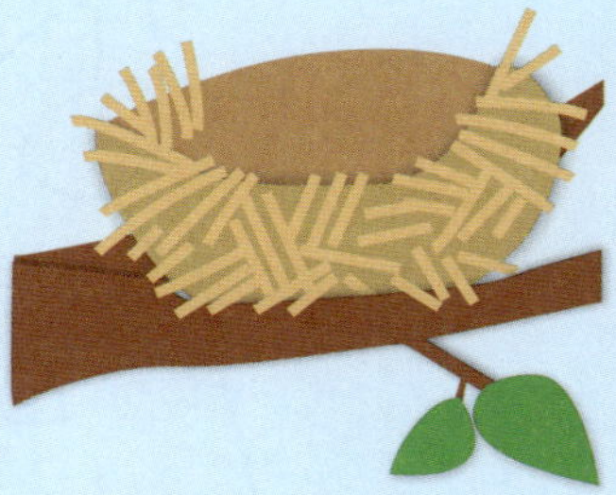

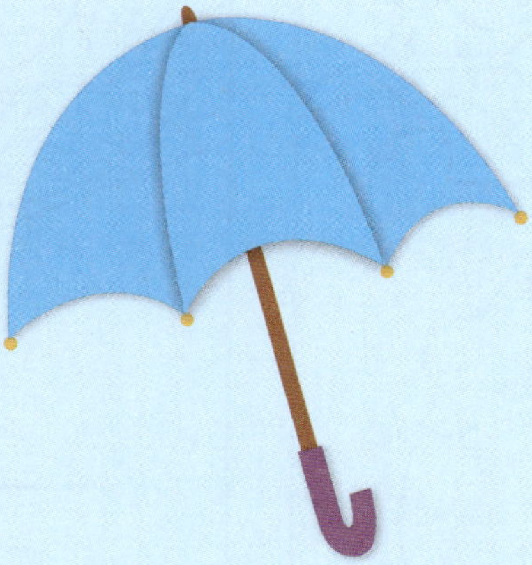

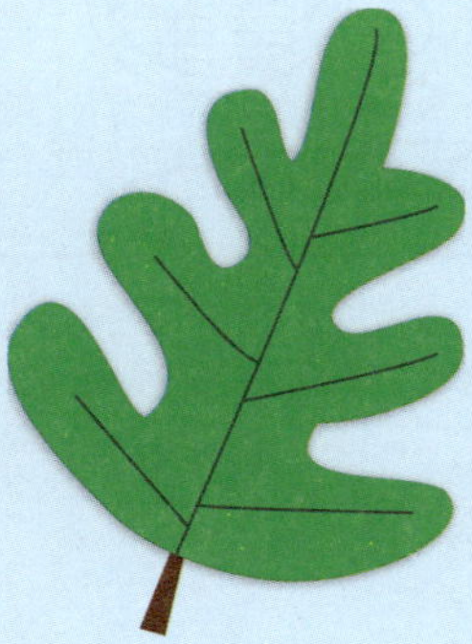

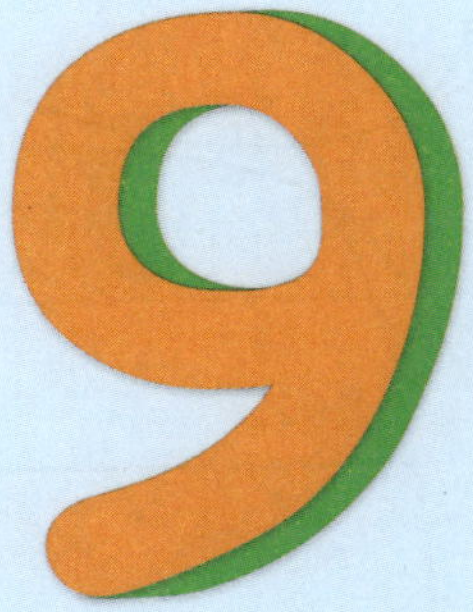

Picture names—*nuts, nest, umbrella, leaf, nine*

Skills: Write upper- and lowercase letters; Fine motor skills; Visual discrimination

Write It!

Trace the letters.

Find the big **N** and the little **n**.
Circle them.

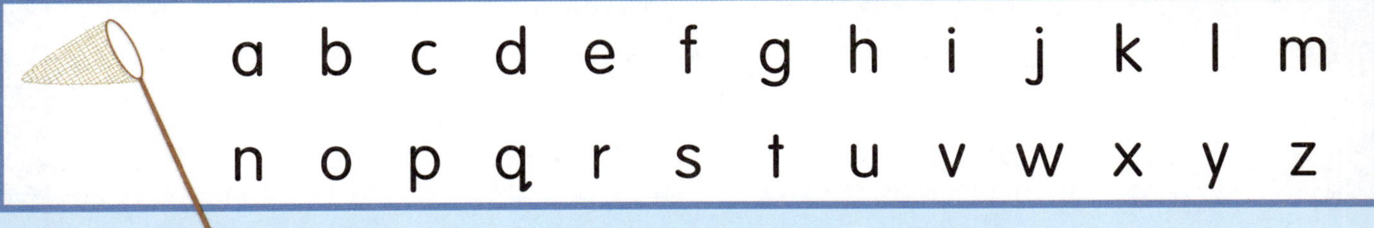

Skills: Visual discrimination; Discriminate beginning sounds; Fine motor skills

Find It!

Circle the letters that are the same as the first letter.

N	F	N	A	N
n	n	n	m	r

Draw something that begins with the letter **n**.

Let's Review!

Trace the letters.

Name the picture.
Color it if it begins like **nightingale**.

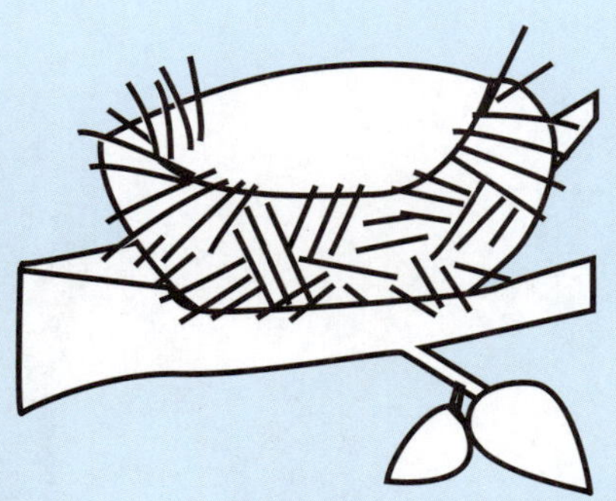

Picture names—*nest, nine, umbrella*

Ollie the Otter

Listen to the story about Ollie the otter. Track 16
Listen for words that begin with the letter **o**.

Ollie is a little otter who lives in the sea. Ollie's mother takes care of him. She carries him on her chest while she floats on her back. She cleans his fur and feeds him tasty bits of clams from the bottom of the sea. Every day, Ollie practices swimming and diving. Today, Ollie dove all the way to the bottom of the sea. He brought back a pretty rock for his mother. Ollie's mom was proud of her little otter.

Color the picture.

Skills: Discriminate beginning sounds; Fine motor skills

Listen for It!

Name the picture.
Circle it if it begins with the same sound as **otter**.

Picture names—*table, dog, octopus, ostrich, bear*

Skills: Write upper- and lowercase letters; Fine motor skills; Visual discrimination

Write It!

Trace the letters.

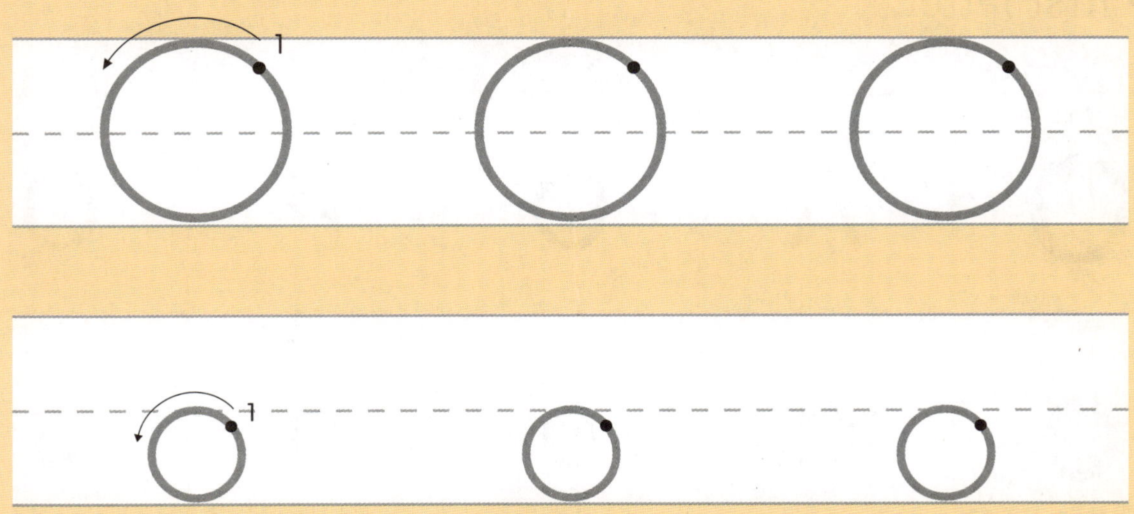

Find the big **O** and the little **o**.
Circle them.

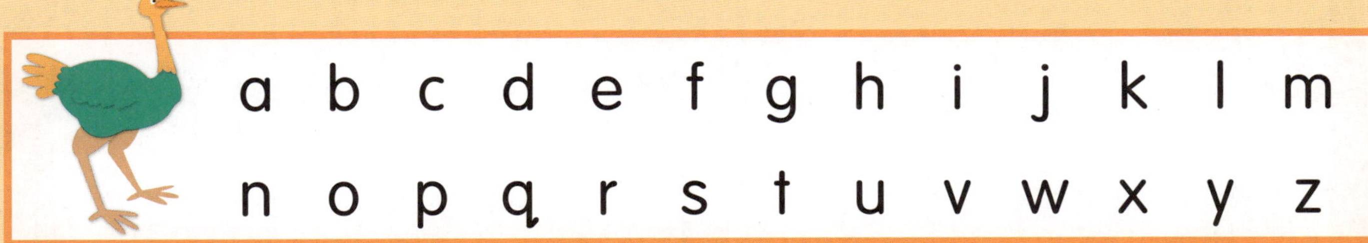

Skills: Visual discrimination; Discriminate beginning sounds; Fine motor skills

Find It!

Circle the letters that are the same as the first letter.

O	A	O	P	O
o	a	o	o	c

Draw and Write

Draw something that begins with the letter **o**.

Skills: Write upper- and lowercase letters; Discriminate beginning sounds

Let's Review!

Trace the letters.

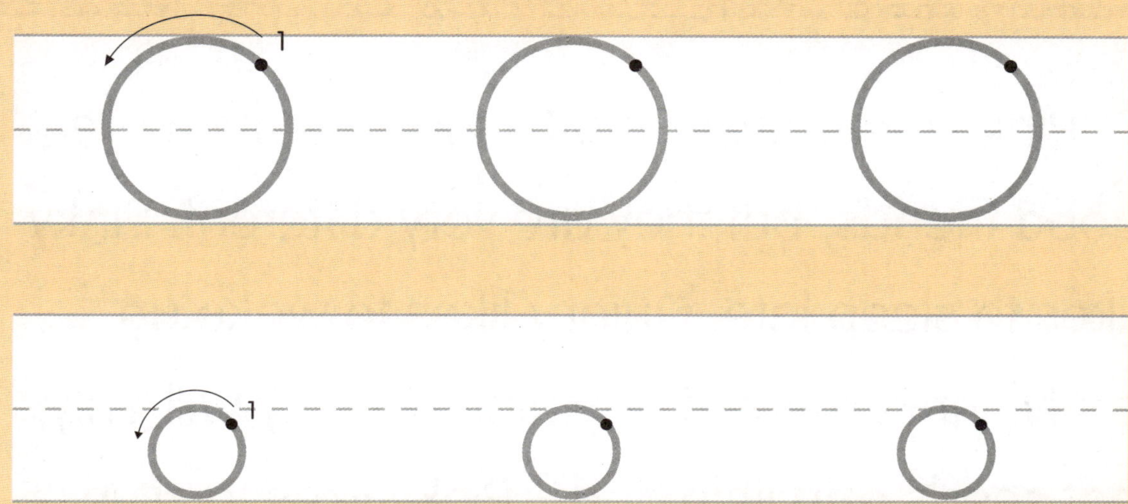

Name the picture.
Color it if it begins like **otter**.

Picture names—*ostrich, table, octopus*

Pinky and Quincy

Listen to the story about Pinky and Quincy. Track 17
Listen for words that begin with the letters **p** and **q**.

Pinky the panda and Quincy the quail are good friends, but they are very different. Pinky likes to sleep late. Quincy likes to wake up early. Pinky will eat anything. Quincy will only eat seeds and little bugs. Pinky likes to sit in mud. Quincy likes to sit in dry dirt. Pinky likes to paint pictures. Quincy likes to sew quilts. Oh well, good friends don't have to like all the same things. They just have to like each other!

Color the picture.

Skills: Discriminate beginning sounds; Fine motor skills

Listen for It!

Name the picture.
Circle it if it begins with the same sound as **panda** or **quail**.

Pp

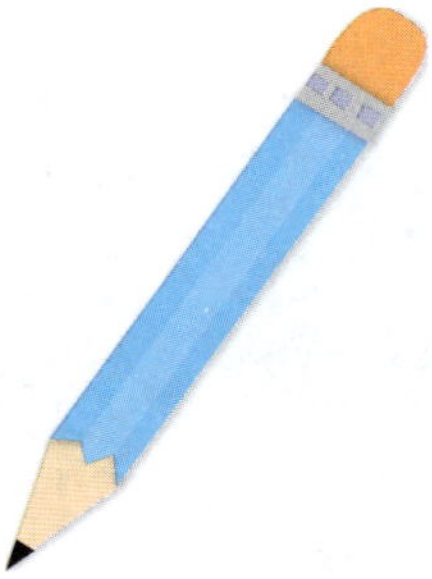

Qq

Picture names—*pie, feather, pumpkin, pencil; quarter, queen, dinosaur, question*

Skills: Write upper- and lowercase letters; Fine motor skills; Visual discrimination

Write It!

Trace the letters.

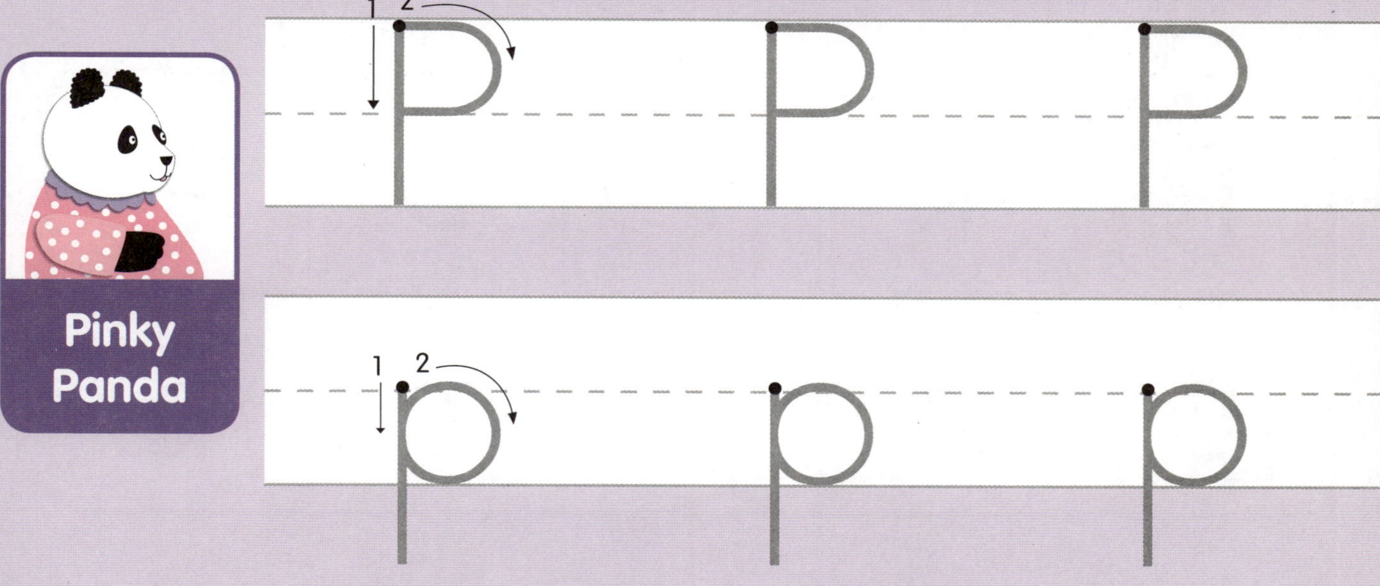

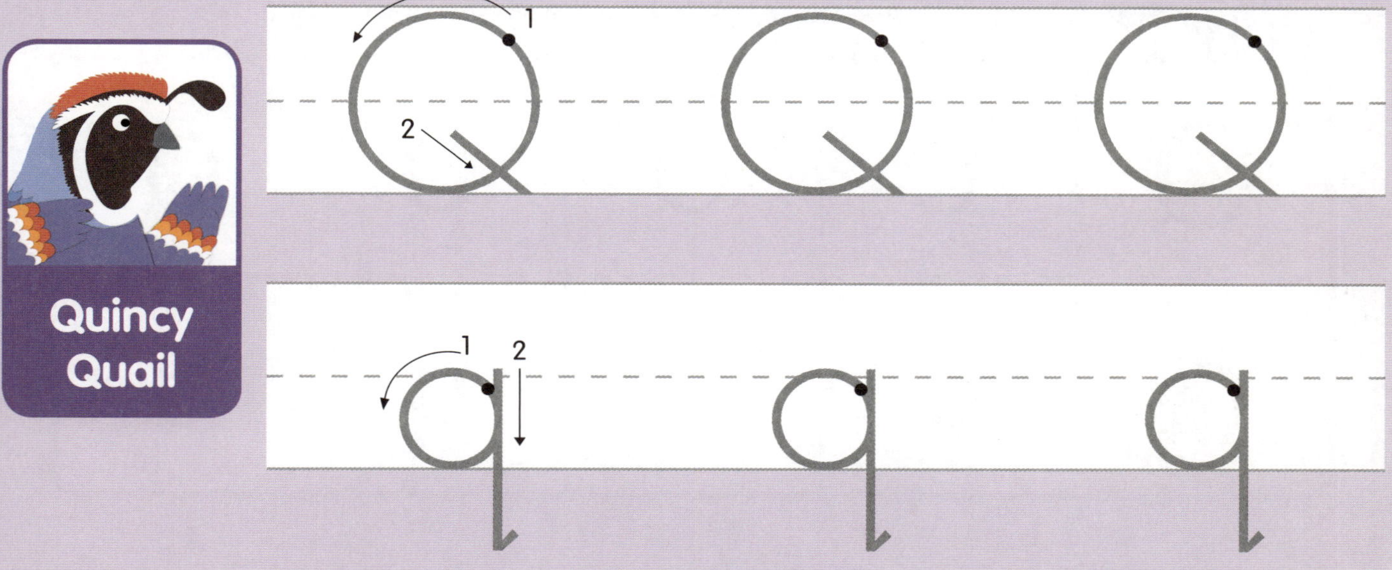

Skills: Visual discrimination; Discriminate beginning sounds; Fine motor skills

Find It!

Circle the letters that are the same as the first letter.

P	R	P	D	P
p	b	p	c	p

Circle the letters that are the same as the first letter.

Q	C	Q	O	Q
q	q	c	q	d

Skills: Write upper- and lowercase letters; Discriminate beginning sounds

Let's Review!

Trace the letters. Name the picture.
Color it if it begins like **panda** or **quail**.

Pinky Panda

Picture names—*pie, feather, pencil*

Quincy Quail

Picture names—*queen, dinosaur, question*

Rosie and Skippy

Listen to the story about Rosie and Skippy. Track 18
Listen for words that begin with the letters **r** and **s**.

Rosie the rabbit looked up at the sun shining through the cloudy sky and said, "This looks like a good day for a picnic." She invited Skippy the skunk to a picnic in the park. Skippy looked at the clouds in the sky and asked, "Are you sure it's a good day for a picnic? It looks like it might rain." Rosie replied, "It will not rain." So Skippy made sandwiches and salad, and he and Rosie went to the park. As soon as they sat down, they felt drops of water on their fur. They looked up at the sky, but neither of them could see a thing—it was raining too hard.

Color the picture.

Skills: Discriminate beginning sounds; Fine motor skills

Listen for It!

Name the picture.
Circle it if it begins with the same sound as **rabbit** or **sun**.

Picture names—*rain, pie, rake, rat; sock, apple, six, sandwich*

Skills: Write upper- and lowercase letters; Fine motor skills; Visual discrimination

Write It!

Trace the letters.

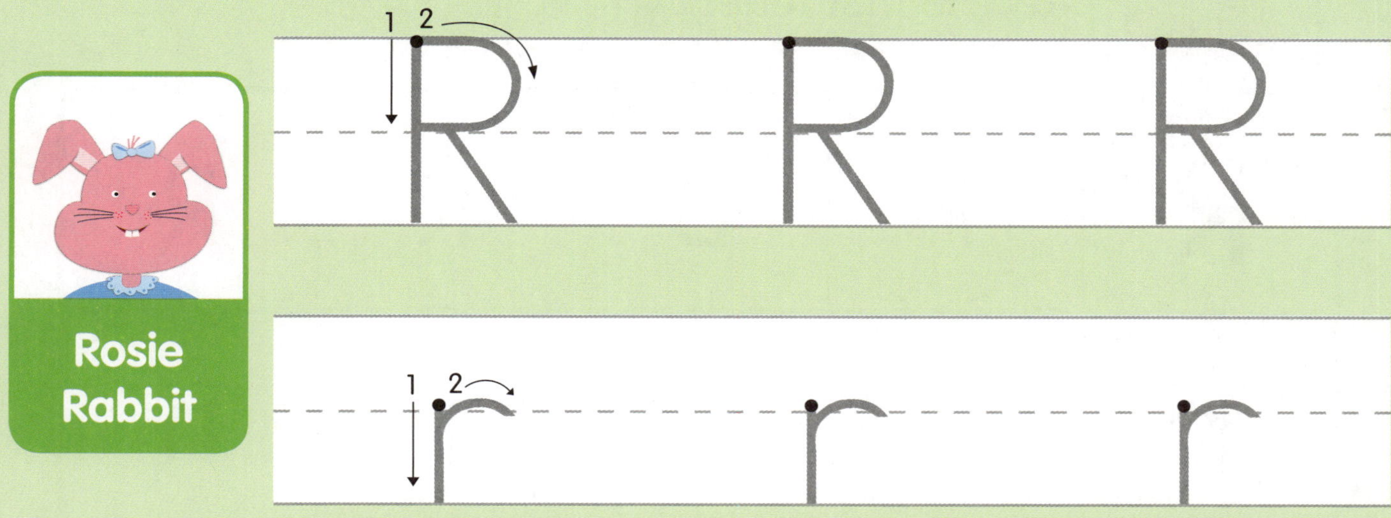

Skills: Visual discrimination; Discriminate beginning sounds; Fine motor skills

Find It!

Circle the letters that are the same as the first letter.

R	F	B	R	R
r	r	c	r	n

Circle the letters that are the same as the first letter.

S	C	S	S	B
s	s	m	s	o

Skills: Write upper- and lowercase letters; Discriminate beginning sounds

Let's Review!

Trace the letters. Name the picture.
Color it if it begins like **rabbit** or **sun**.

Picture names—*rat, pie, rain*

Picture names—*sock, six, apple*

Tootie and Uncle Buck

Listen to the story about Tootie and Uncle Buck. Track 19
Listen for words that begin with the letters **t** and **u**.

Tootie the turtle and Uncle Buck like to watch television on rainy days. One Saturday, Tootie called Uncle Buck on the telephone. "Hi, Uncle Buck. Are you watching television today?" asked Tootie. "Just a minute, Tootie. I'll go look up at the sky," said Uncle Buck. "Come on over. It looks like it's going to rain," he said. "I'll be right over," said Tootie. She grabbed her umbrella, put on her rain hat, and walked out the door.

Sure enough, before she got there, it started to rain. "Oh good," said Tootie, "I love rainy Saturdays!"

Color the picture.

Name the picture.
Circle it if it begins with the same sound as **turtle** or **uncle.**

Tt

Uu

Picture names—*telephone, tent, jeep, tie; unhappy, kitten, umbrella, up*

Trace the letters.

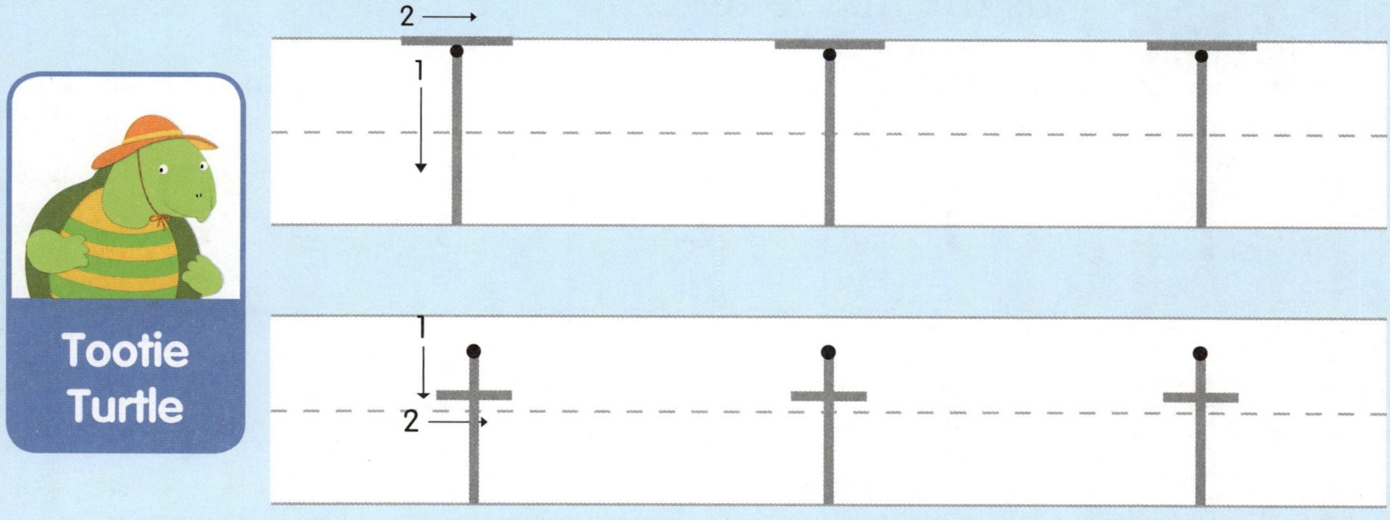

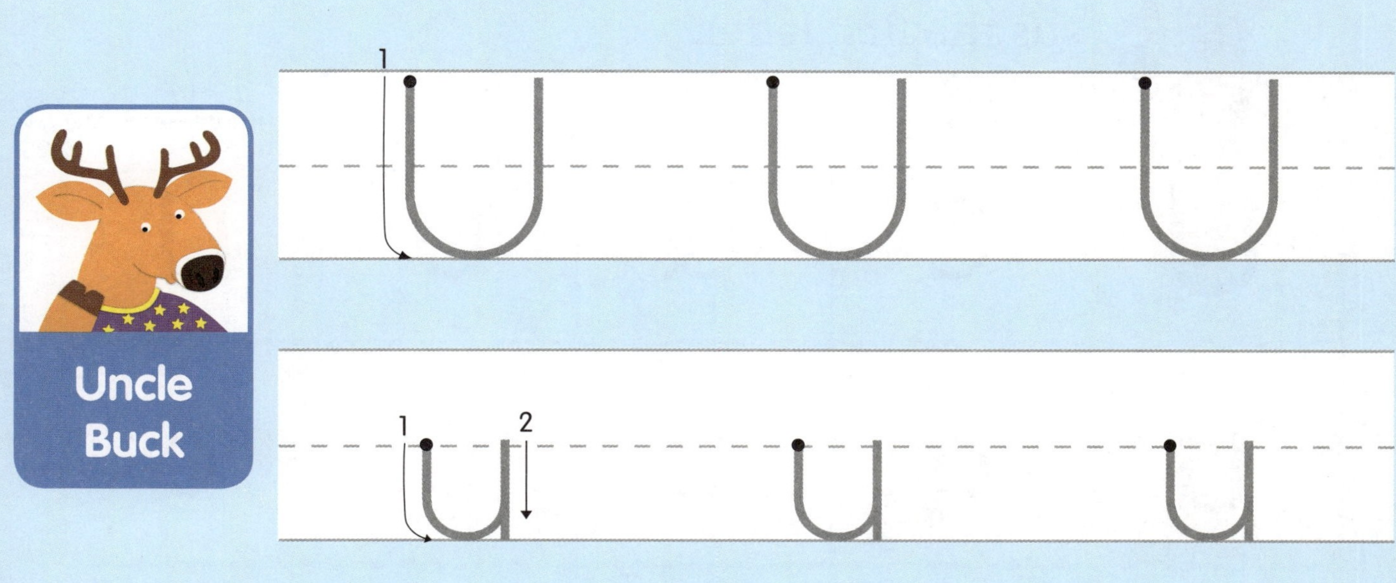

Circle the letters that are the same as the first letter.

T	T	L	T	P
t	t	x	t	i

Circle the letters that are the same as the first letter.

U	C	Q	U	U
u	q	u	u	c

Skills: Write upper- and lowercase letters; Discriminate beginning sounds

Let's Review!

Trace the letters. Name the picture.
Color it if it begins like **turtle** or **uncle**.

Tootie Turtle

Picture names—*tie, jeep, tent*

Uncle Buck

Picture names—*umbrella, up, kitten*

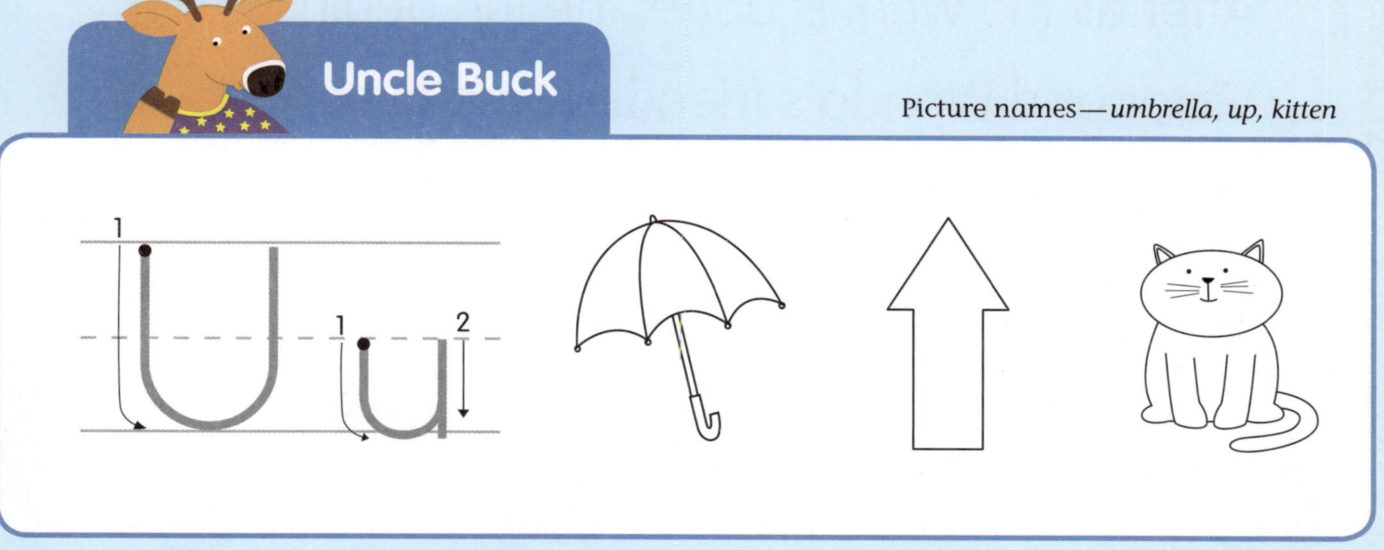

Victor and Wanda

Listen to the story about Victor and Wanda. Track 20
Listen for words that begin with the letters **v** and **w**.

Victor the vulture and Wanda the walrus are having a party today. Victor and Wanda like having parties, but parties sure are a lot of work! Wanda has to vacuum the rugs and wash the windows. Victor has to pull the watermelons off the vines and slice them. Then he has to polish and tune his violin. After all the work is done, the fun begins. Victor and Wanda's friends come over and dance and sing and eat.

Color the picture.

Skills: Discriminate beginning sounds; Fine motor skills

Listen for It!

Name the picture. Circle it if it begins with the same sound as **vulture** or **walrus**.

Vv

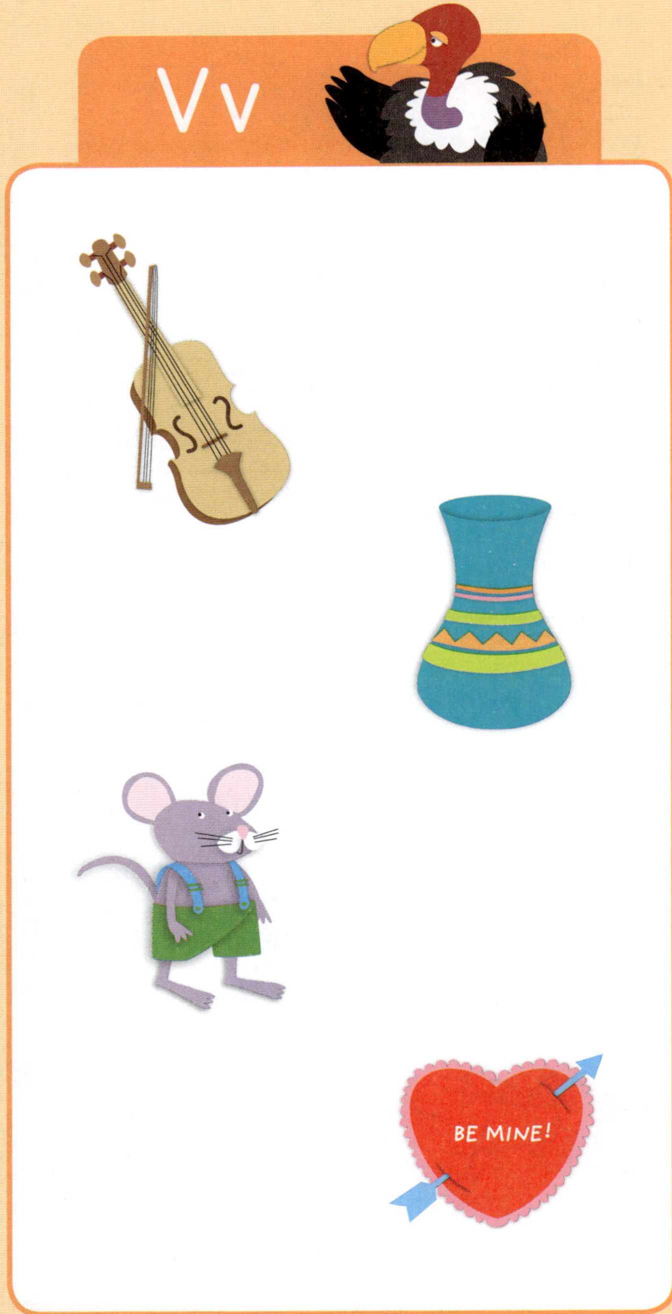

Ww

Picture names—*violin, vase, mouse, valentine; web, kite, wagon, watermelon*

Skills: Write upper- and lowercase letters; Fine motor skills; Visual discrimination

Write It!

Trace the letters.

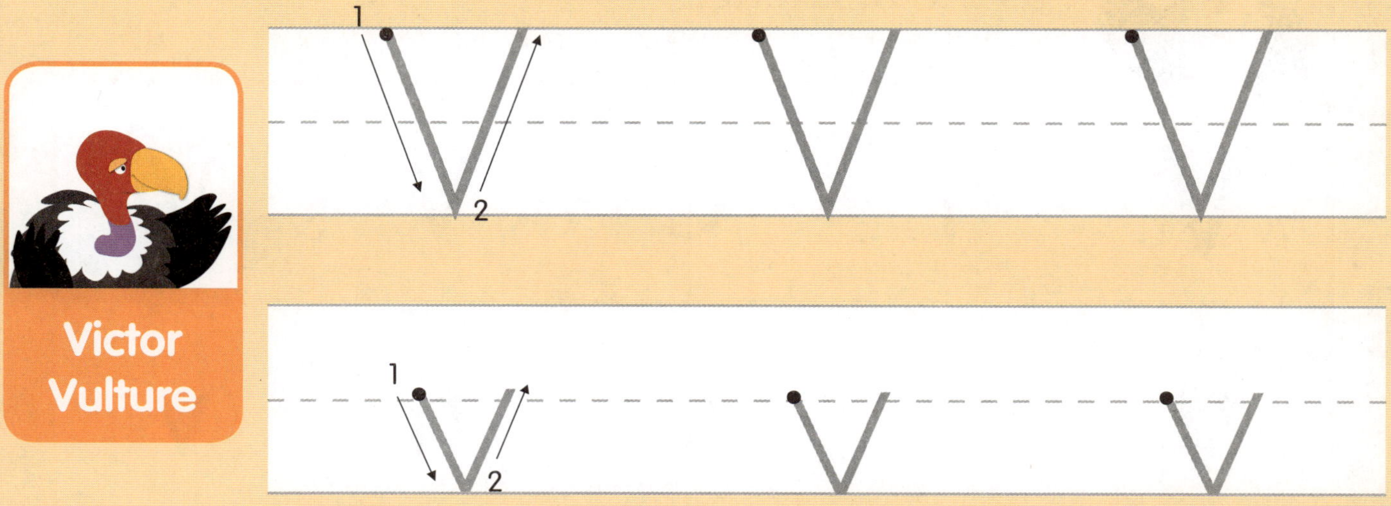

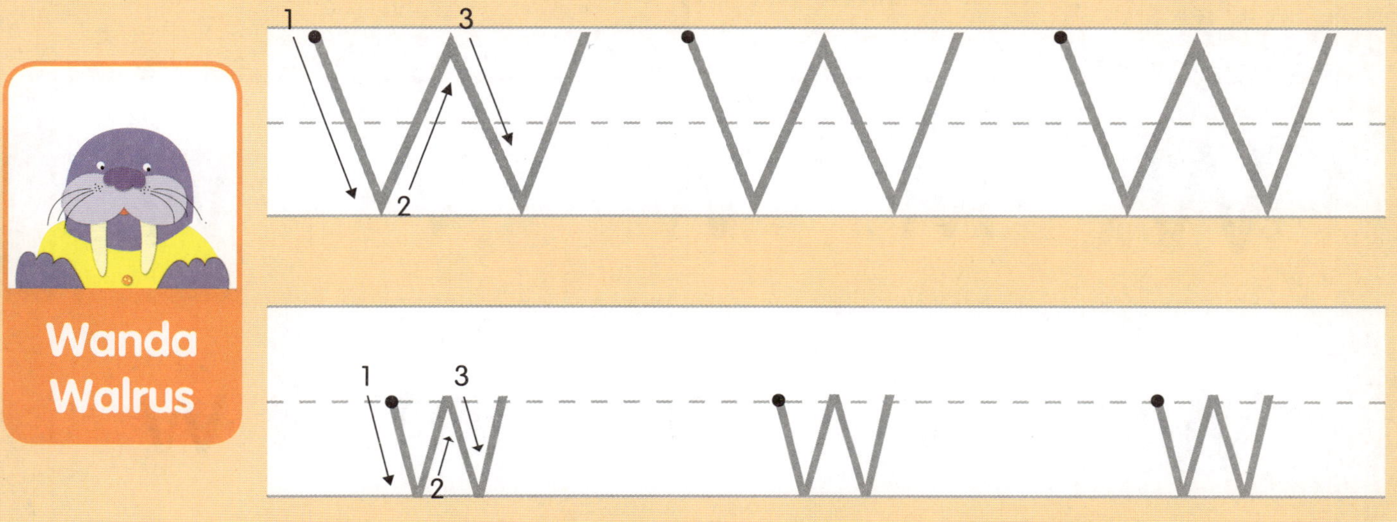

Skills: Visual discrimination; Discriminate beginning sounds; Fine motor skills

Find It!

Circle the letters that are the same as the first letter.

V	T	C	V	V
v	r	v	n	v

Circle the letters that are the same as the first letter.

W	M	W	V	W
w	w	n	m	w

Skills: Write upper- and lowercase letters; Discriminate beginning sounds

Let's Review!

Trace the letters. Name the picture.
Color it if it begins like **vulture** or **walrus**.

Victor Vulture

Picture names—*violin, vase, mouse*

Wanda Walrus

Picture names—*wagon, kite, web*

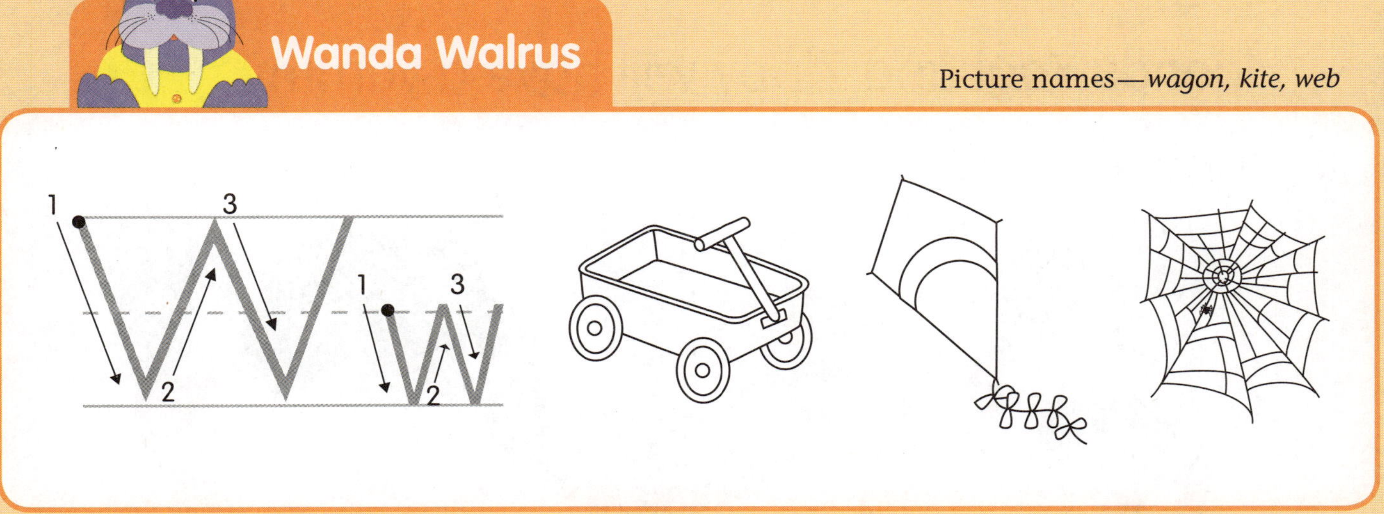

Roxie, Yogi, and Zippy

Listen to the story about Roxie, Yogi, and Zippy. Track 21
Listen for words that end in **x** and begin with **y** and **z**.

Roxie the fox is an excellent cook. She loves to try new recipes and invite her friends over for lunch. Today, Yogi the yak and Zippy the zebra are going to Roxie's house for lunch. Roxie is making a delicious vegetable soup. It has broccoli, carrots, and zucchini in it. Then she will mix up some homemade frozen yogurt with chocolate chips for dessert. Her friends Yogi and Zippy will have a yummy lunch!

Color the picture.

Skills: Discriminate beginning and ending sounds; Fine motor skills

Listen for It!

Name the picture. Circle it if it <u>ends</u> with the same sound as **fox.**

Picture names—*ax, cup, ox*

Name the picture. Circle it if it begins with the same sound as **yak.**

Picture names—*yo-yo, yogurt, umbrella*

Name the picture. Circle it if it begins with the same sound as **zebra.**

Picture names—*zipper, bat, zero*

Skills: Write upper- and lowercase letters; Fine motor skills; Visual discrimination

Write It!

Trace the letters.

Roxie Fox

X X X

x x x

Yogi Yak

Y Y Y

y y y

Zippy Zebra

Z Z Z

z z z

Skills: Visual discrimination; Discriminate beginning and ending sounds; Fine motor skills

Find It!

Circle the letters that are the same as the first letter.

X	T	M	X	X
x	r	x	p	x

Y	Y	M	P	Y
y	x	y	y	w

Z	Z	N	Z	L
z	z	r	y	z

Skills: Write upper- and lowercase letters; Discriminate beginning and ending sounds

Let's Review!

Trace the letters. Name the picture.
Color it if it ends like **fox** or begins like **yak** or **zebra**.

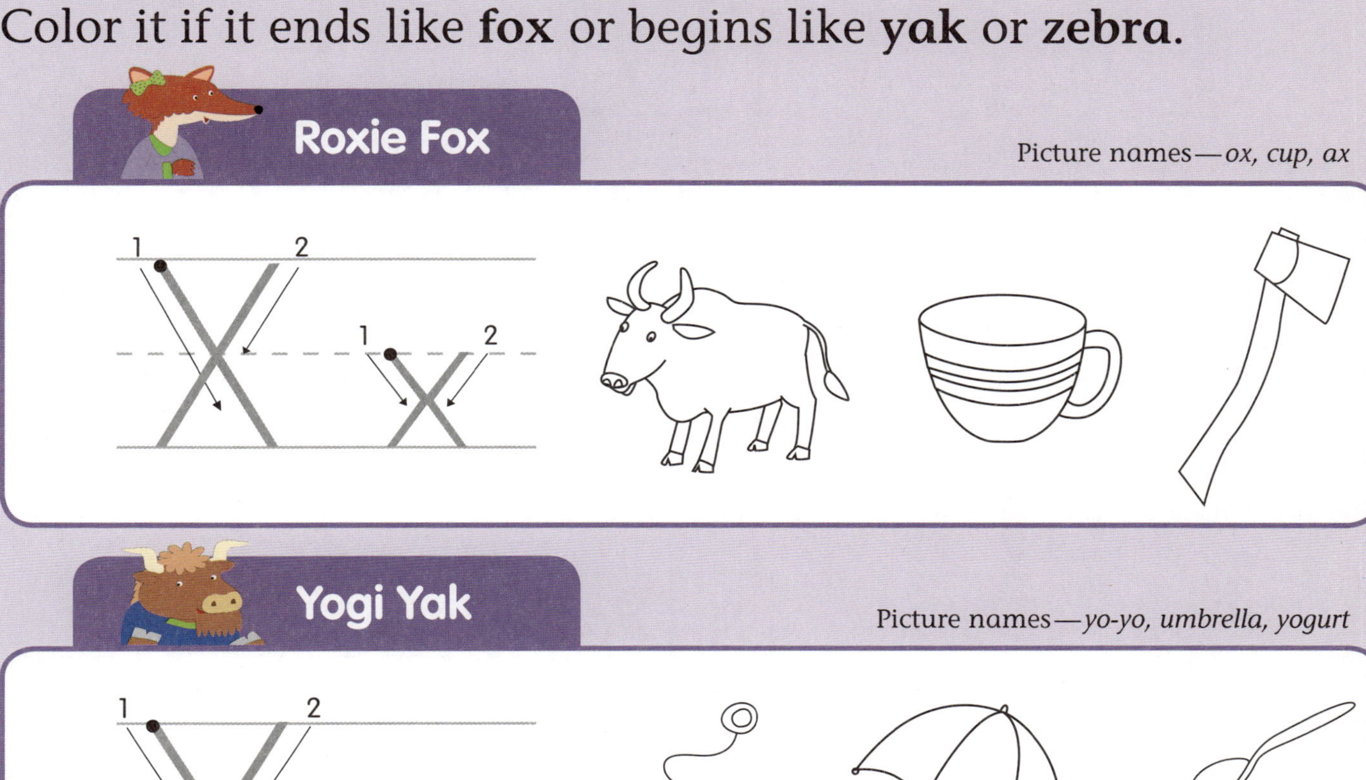

Roxie Fox

Picture names—*ox, cup, ax*

Yogi Yak

Picture names—*yo-yo, umbrella, yogurt*

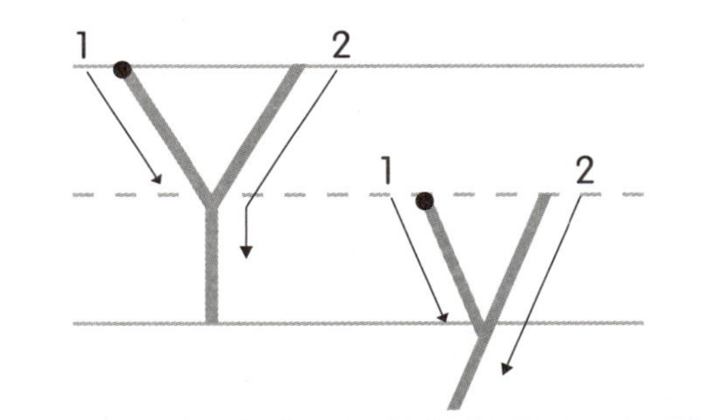
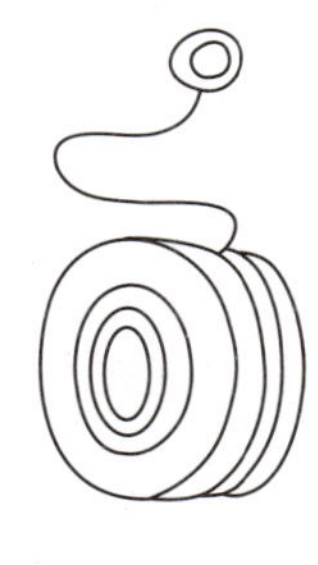

Zippy Zebra

Picture names—*bat, zero, zipper*

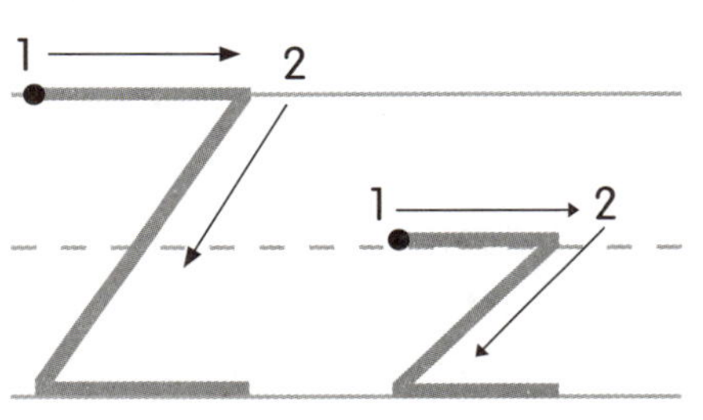

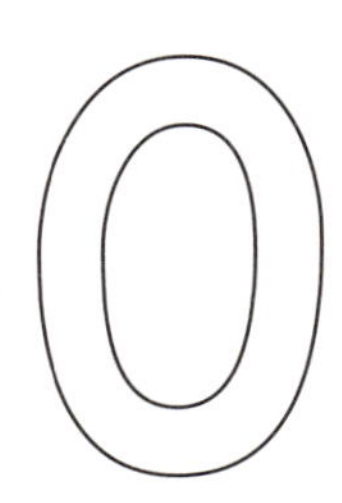
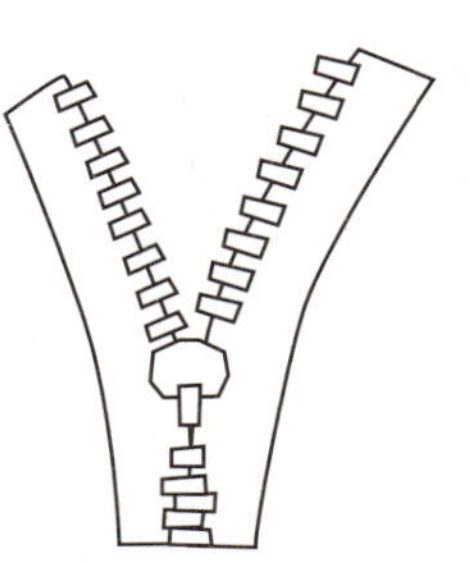

Alphabet Trace

Answer Key

Page 8
Circled pictures: apple, alligator, anthill

Page 11
Colored pictures: apple, alligator

Page 14
Circled pictures: bat, bed, boat

Page 17
Colored pictures: bat, bed

Page 20
Circled pictures: cup, corn, cane

Page 23
Colored pictures: cup, corn

Page 26
Circled pictures: door, dinosaur, duck

Page 29
Colored pictures: duck, door

Page 32
Circled pictures: eggs, elbow, envelope

Page 35
Colored pictures: elbow, envelope

Page 38
Circled pictures: feather, five, fox

Page 41
Colored pictures: feather, fox

Page 44
Circled pictures: gate, guitar, goat

Page 47
Colored pictures: goat, gate

Page 50
Circled pictures: hat, house, horse

Page 53
Colored pictures: hat, house

Page 56
Circled pictures: insects, itch, igloo

Page 59
Colored pictures: igloo, insects

Page 62
Circled pictures: jeep, jam, jet

Page 65
Colored pictures: jam, jet

Page 68
Circled pictures: kitten, key, king

Page 71
Colored pictures: key, kite

Page 74
Circled pictures: ladder, lion, leaf

Page 77
Colored pictures: lion, leaf

Page 80

Circled pictures: moon, monkey, mittens

Page 83

Colored pictures: mittens, monkey

Page 86

Circled pictures: nuts, nest, nine

Page 89

Colored pictures: nest, nine

Page 92

Circled pictures: octopus, ostrich

Page 95

Colored pictures: ostrich, octopus

Page 98

Circled pictures: pie, pumpkin, pencil; quarter, queen, question

Page 101

Colored pictures: pie, pencil; queen, question

Page 104

Circled pictures: rain, rake, rat; sock, six, sandwich

Page 107

Colored pictures: rat, rain; sock, six

Page 110

Circled pictures: telephone, tent, tie; unhappy, umbrella, up

Page 113

Colored pictures: tie, tent; umbrella, up

Page 116

Circled pictures: violin, vase, valentine; web, wagon, watermelon

Page 119

Colored pictures: violin, vase; wagon, web

Page 122

Circled pictures: ax, ox; yo-yo, yogurt; zipper, zero

Page 125

Colored pictures: ox, ax; yo-yo, yogurt; zero, zipper

WOW!
Hooray
Yay!
Fun!
Woof!
Boom!
WOW!
Hooray
Yay!
Fun!
Woof!
Boom!
WOW!
Hooray
Yay!
Fun!
Woof!
Boom!
WOW!
Hooray
Yay!
Fun!
Woof!
Boom!
Bam!
Wham!
Yes!
Brilliant!
Excellent
I Rock!
Bam!
Wham!
Yes!
Brilliant!
Excellent
I Rock!
Bam!
Wham!
Yes!
Brilliant!
Excellent
I Rock!
Bam!
Wham!
Yes!
Brilliant!
Excellent
I Rock!